GREAT BRAND STORIES

GUINNESS IS GUINNESS
THE COLOURFUL STORY OF
A BLACK AND WHITE BRAND

MARK GRIFFITHS

For Debs and Stan and the Dream

Copyright © 2005 Mark Griffiths

First published in Great Britain in 2004 by
Cyan Books, an imprint of

Cyan Communications Limited
4.3 The Ziggurat
60–66 Saffron Hill
London EC1N 8QX
www.cyanbooks.com

This updated edition published in 2005

The right of Mark Griffiths to be identifiied
as the author of this work has been asserted
by him in accordance with the Copyright,
Designs and Patents Act 1988.

A CIP record for this book is available
from the British Library

ISBN 1-904879-28-4

Printed and bound in Great Britain
by TJ International, Padstow, Cornwall

CONTENTS

PREFACE

Mark Griffiths is a self-confessed adorer of Guinness. When I asked him if he would be interested in writing this book he "bit my hand off" (his words). The passion he feels for Guinness can be tasted in every word of this book. Mark is a writer of strong opinions and surging words. Read him and you start to sense something even deeper in what Guinness terms "inner strength." The style is pure Guinness: powerful, engaging, at times surreal, but always ready to share a good story.

Mark has written the story of the Guinness brand, but this is no company history. Go with the flow of the book and you'll find out about the people and events that have made Guinness the brand it is today: revered around the world by drinkers and non-drinkers alike. Guinness has been going strong since 1759, and I can think of very few brands of such longevity. After 250 years, Guinness continues to inspire loyalty and commitment; and still you feel there is so much more to come.

If you're interested in Guinness; if you want to learn lessons from one great brand to shine a light on another; if you want to read a good story... read on.

John Simmons
Series editor, *Great brand stories*

PLANET GUINNESS

I adore Guinness. Guinness wasn't my first love, nor I its. We both had to work hard to kindle the flame. It's been a slow-burning passion.

The words "adore" and "passion" are very important to Guinness. Guinness passionately wants all its consumers to become adorers. When you become a Guinness Adorer you see the world in black and white for ever, even though not all of it makes sense. Sometimes Guinness advertising may seem to be talking to other people, but it will be sure to come back to you later. Besides, you'll be looking down the ladder of commitment, quietly calling to mere Guinness Adopters and Accepters, "Come on up – life's creamy at the top."

Everyone has their favourite Guinness advert. Everyone remembers their first Guinness advert. Everyone talks about Guinness adverts from time to time. Or that's the belief at Guinness – and the Guinness brand people understand belief and do their research meticulously. It's been that way for 75 years of Guinness advertising. But 75 years is nothing in comparison with about 250 years of living Guinness history. OK, it's 30 percent. A bit more than the amount still remaining to be poured after the surge has settled.

But it's easy to digress. So much Guinness history, so much to talk about. My point is this: in a world that increasingly judges international brands in terms of the negative impact of globalization, Guinness is almost unique in the way it's been perceived around the world, especially as a drinks company.

It has been welcomed everywhere, even in Muslim countries. Why has Guinness been impervious to the cultural colonialism that seems to personify the activity of other major food and drinks brands? If it isn't your health, what *is* it about Guinness that's good for you?

Guinness is a beer that troubles some American commentators. "You can't sell black beer in a blond market," said one about a particular Guinness attempt to market itself to American customers at the end of the last century. In fact, when the black beer with an Irish home arrived in America two centuries ago, its market was already there. Irish Americans wanted the real McCoy. And they got it – transported all the way to the saloon bars of New York and Boston on the White Star Liners.

Yet today, when Guinness is brewed on the continent itself, the US is only Guinness's fourth largest market. Given its struggle in the crowded contemporary marketplace, you'd think it was a new kid on the block. Does heritage count for nothing? For sure, Guinness is anything but a parochial Irish beer. But the fact that a beer has been around for a quarter of a century does not make it a brand that has a right to stay around for another quarter of a decade or sell one more pint in America.

Today, Guinness clearly has some difficult marketing issues to address – not the least its approach to corporate social responsibility. As a 250-year-old brand, it also has some incredibly useful knowledge to impart to a wide audience: from brand managers to students of advertising, business consultants to armchair philosophers, the pub wag expounding on the meaning of life to the doctor prepared to offer alternative remedies (joke). A lot of people have done a lot of good with this brand.

I was born in the month when Guinness celebrated its 200th anniversary, June 1959. If I ever get to mark my century in the year that Guinness begins its fourth, it won't be down to too little of the black stuff. Yet this is no hagiography or sentimental appreciation. It's not an internal brand job masquerading as a balanced view. In this independent book, I set out to show at several levels why Guinness is more than just a simple beer, and I have some tough questions to ask.

I've been working with Guinness for several years, first through a creative agency and since as an independent writer. I understand the brand, where it's come from, what it's trying to achieve. Now I'd like to share with you some of the reasons why I believe Guinness is one of the truly global brands in existence today.

I may be an Adorer, but I want to get to the bottom of the glass. As The Man with the Guinness in the surreal TV ad that got me hooked once said, "It's not easy being a dolphin."

And it's not easy being my wife. My deep thanks go to Debbie, first for putting up with a complete boor in the months of October, November and December 2003, when I was researching and writing this book; second for her editing skills, for finding the book within. Apparently we moved house during that time and there were lots of problems. Out went personal hygiene and any consideration for another living being. I became an irresponsible drinker; I didn't buy anyone a round. How irresponsible can you get?

I felt and looked like Forrest Gump running around America. I was on Planet Guinness, in my own special world.

Speaking of special worlds, when Dan McAuliffe gave me a personal tour around the hidden parts of Dublin's St James's Gate Brewery that nobody sees and that he's known man and boy, I surprised him now and again by stopping and putting my hands on the ancient walls, or running my fingers over the flagstones, or sniffing the dank air of a disused delivery tunnel. Although I listened to his stories of decades, I made no notes. All I wanted to do was absorb the mystery of the place. I allowed Dan's fine descriptions to wash through me. Some of them are untellable by anyone else. After two hours of walking through brewhouses old and new, through kegging plants, past fire station and bank, and by numerous nooks and crannies where the carpenters and joiners used to work, or meet to drink their free portion from taps, I felt I knew something I didn't know before. I was sure I had absorbed something of the secret ingredient that Arthur Guinness brewed into his stout and that makes Guinness taste like nothing else. But when I left the brewery, I just could not say what it was. Some of it, I hope, is in this book.

I'd like to thank the following people at Guinness who indulged me by answering my questions for this book or helped me in other ways: Jon Potter, David Cunningham, Mark Ody, John Wheelhouse, Adrian Green, Aine Friel, Rhonda Bollard, Anne O'Sullivan, Neil Skinner, Dan McAuliffe, Mike Crawford and Kate Blakeley. Thank you to Lisa McElhinney, Eibhlin Roche and Clare Hackett in the Diageo archives in Menstrie, Scotland and the Guinness Storehouse in Dublin.

Not forgetting Cecile Beaufils, Magnus Blair and Jo Clarke from Abbott Mead Vickers BBDO and Nozi Sishuba and Tony Dunseath from Saatchi's, Guinness's advertising agencies in the UK and South Africa respectively. Special thanks for the use of Guinness photography in Ireland, Malaysia and Ghana to Glyn Genin and Jeff Jones.

I'd like to thank the following people who have moved on from their time with Guinness but gave me valuable insights into their work: Francis Eames, Alan Wood, Brian Pate, Jon Eggleton, Neil Quick, Neil Cassie and Michael Constantinidi. At least one of these people said: "Guinness is Guinness. You can read too much into it." Well, I hope so.

This book would not have been possible without authors before me who have also tried to make sense in black and white: Edward Guinness, Jonathan Guinness, Michele Guinness, Derek Wilson, Brian Sibley and Jim Davies.

Almost last, but not least, I'd like to thank John Simmons, editor of this *Great brand stories* series, who recommended me for this book, and with whom I've worked for years, not least on the Guinness account. Thanks go to my publishers, Martin Liu, for his understanding and support, and Pom Somkabcharti, for her unswerving determination to get this book to print.

Last, thank goodness for Guinness.

IN
DRINKING
GUINNESS

You walk into a pub. See a beer on the bar. It's black and bitter, like mud in a glass. You're 18 years old and none of your mates drinks it, so why should you? Yet there's something strangely attractive about it. Never mind. There's no time to wait. Another day, maybe. You've got your whole life ahead of you.

How did you see Guinness when you were 18?

A brand is simply a series of beliefs in your head. Only some of them are based on knowledge. You don't know a lot when you're 18, even though you think you do. What you don't know won't hurt you, but it will hurt the brand – which is why the brand works extra hard to increase your knowledge base. Guinness has been working very hard on your education since before you were born.

Guinness is not like most beer brands. It knows that its distinctiveness means you can see it coming and can't be fooled. Besides, it's always been true to itself. It knows that, even though you haven't tried it, you think you know all there is to know about it. It can't help being different. Guinness just is. But it's not as black and white as that.

STREAM OF GUINNESSNESS

You might actually have tried the drink, but you would never ever try it again under any circumstances. As far as Guinness is concerned, you're a brand Rejecter. It prays there aren't many around like you. But unless you're a staunch Rejecter, there is a glimmer of hope. After all, you probably won't have tried it in the right circumstances. Besides, you don't really know much about it. Perhaps it has registered on your radar, but you still don't know enough about it to try it. Guinness sees you as ripe and open for persuasion. Whether you realize it or not, you've got one foot on the ladder.

You are **Available**. If only you knew a little more, you might get interested. Something about the brand might attract you to try it. You'd like to, but maybe you're just waiting for the right opportunity. Is Guinness the right drink for you? What does it taste like? Once you've dipped your toe in the dark water, it's not so bad after all. It's not a beer you tend to drink, but every now and again you'll have one. After all, you're open to new experiences, as long as people don't judge you by them. Will it make you stand out like a sore thumb? On the other hand, someone said it's great with a shot of Tia Maria in it.

You're an **Accepter**. But then again, why worry too much? Things settle down in life and you know you like a Guinness as long as you're not in a rush. You work hard and there's your reward. Now you can relax with your occasional Guinness. And now that life's sorted out, it becomes a kind of pleasant habit. You know what you're like and what you like. Guinness is even becoming a regular, one of your favourites. As long as you can get it in your local and they serve it properly, the way it should be.

You're an **Adopter**. You can get serious about getting a perfect pint of Guinness. And why not? You've spent a good while acquiring the taste, and it's been well worth it. You're going to remain loyal. You'll make a point about ordering a Guinness in most places, as a matter of principle. And, boy, they'd better pour it right or you'll have something to say. You can identify with what Guinness stands for and you know what it says about you. You feel highly individual and yet, strangely, part of a secret club. You know something that other people don't. Why would you want to drink any other brand?

You're a confirmed **Adorer**.

AVAILABLE, ACCEPTER, ADOPTER, ADORER

The people who make and market Guinness today are very interested in how you see the beer, whether you drink it, how much of it you drink, and when and where you drink it.

This and other messages throughout the book were left on the "Home" wall of postcards by visitors to the Guinness Storehouse in Dublin, 28 November 2003.

They want to encourage you to try it, then drink more, but responsibly. They work hard at confirming your acceptance and dispelling your prejudices, because you have both.

13

A perfect pint of Guinness

You might be 25, 45, somewhere in between or either side. From your point of view, Guinness has certain things going for it that draw you in or push you away. But it isn't as black and white as that. We don't just adore or reject it. There are stages in between. You and I might call it acquiring the taste. At Guinness, they call it the "ladder of commitment" and they're very interested in where you are on the journey up it.

And how about you? Do you recognize yourself on this ladder? Do you understand how you got there? Perhaps this book will help you understand your personal role among millions in making Guinness the great global brand it is today.

When you look at Guinness, what do you see? The same as you did last week, last year, a decade ago? What is myth and what is truth about Guinness? One thing's for sure, you will already have a view on that. Are you one of those for whom Guinness is Guinness? Or do you belong to those who believe that Guinness is Guinnessness? I hope you're paying attention. I may ask more questions.

But before we hit the myths and legends, you need to take in some stats.

SOME TRUTHS ABOUT GUINNESS

— Guinness is made from four natural ingredients: barley, water, hops and yeast. The dark colour and the unique taste come from the roast barley.

— Around ten million glasses of Guinness are drunk around the world every day.

— The Guinness family has not been directly involved in the management of the company since 1992, although they retain a significant financial interest in the business.

— In 1998, Guinness joined with Grand Metropolitan to form the biggest drinks company in the world: Diageo. Guinness is now the major beer brand among a shelf of spirits including Smirnoff, Bailey's, Johnnie Walker, J&B and others. Guinness itself owns other beers such as Harp lager, Kilkenny, Ireland's Smithwick's ale and Jamaica's Red Stripe lager.

— Guinness is sold in 150 countries around the globe and can be found in such far-flung places as Novosibirsk in central Siberia and Kathmandu in Nepal, which is supplied by the high-altitude Mount Everest Brewery.

— Guinness is brewed in 49 countries, as well as at St James's Gate, Dublin, but its 70 year-old Park Royal brewery in London closes in 2005.

— Guinness is brewed to suit local tastes. In Ireland, Great Britain, the US and Australia, people drink Guinness Draught. In Africa, Asia and the Caribbean they drink Guinness Foreign Extra Stout.

> Guinness
> turns your
> shite black.

Source: Message left on the "Home" wall of postcards by a visitor to the Guinness Storehouse in Dublin, 28 November 2003

— In the UK and the US, people have been drinking Guinness Draught only since the 1960s. Before that, they drank Guinness Extra Stout, also known as Guinness Original.

— Guinness Foreign Extra Stout now accounts for 40 percent of world sales. It has a deep, rich and powerful taste, and the highest alcohol content of any Guinness beer.

— In various parts of the world today you can get Guinness Draught, Guinness Draught Extra Cold, Guinness Draught In Cans, Guinness Draught In Bottles, Guinness Extra Stout, Guinness Original, Guinness Foreign Extra Stout and Guinness Extra Smooth. In Muslim countries you can also get Malta Guinness, a top-selling non-alcoholic drink.

— The top five Guinness markets around the world in sales terms are Great Britain, Ireland, Nigeria, the US and Cameroon. Nigeria will soon overtake Ireland.
— A pint of Guinness has fewer calories than a pint of semi-skimmed milk or a pint of orange juice.

Right, now you're tuned in, let's get on with things.

WIDGET BELIEVE IT?

You know all about the widget, don't you? The British recently voted it the greatest invention in the past 40 years.[1] More important than the Internet. And email. And why not? The Internet is just an electronic noticeboard, and email is for people who've forgotten how to write. Whereas the widget is your permission to drink at home, your route to relaxation, your passport to freedom. (Actually, it's a small plastic device in the bottom of the can that introduces nitrogen into the beer to create a pint just like the one you get down the pub.)

That thing

That's what you mean by innovation. That thing they invented. The tiny, shiny new thingamajig with a minute hole in. They put it in the beer just before they seal the can. The doofer is full of nitrogen but it can't escape because the beer is pressurized with carbon dioxide. When you open the can, the pressure drops and the nitrogen whooshes into the beer and forces it to release dissolved carbon dioxide. And that's how you get the creamy head on top of the beer. The widget did it.

1 Notes appear at the end of each chapter.

Introduced in the UK in 1989, the widget won the Queen's Award for Technological Achievement in 1991. Since then, almost every brewer has copied the technology to produce its own creamy beers and lagers. That's the power of the widget. But as with all Guinness innovations, it took years to get to and was based on commercial necessity. And we're going to see just how crucial innovation and its twin, quality, are in the history of Guinness brand development.

It's tempting to say that, with Guinness Draught Extra Cold and Guinness Draught In Cans and Bottles, never mind Guinness Draught itself, we've seen more innovation in the past 50 years than in 250 years of Guinness history. But it's not true. Guinness has been a brilliant innovator ever since Arthur Guinness took out his 9,000 year lease on St James's Gate Brewery in 1759. That said, innovation and quality are at the heart of the Guinness brand today and there's no shortage of passion to make sure they stay that way.

Walking around the windy, ghostly caverns of Park Royal and St James's Gate in London and Dublin today, you do get that sense of innovation, but one tinged with melancholy. At Park Royal, two shifts of a dozen or so computer-aided men control the entire brewery output around the clock, doing the work of hundreds if not thousands of men before them. Although St James's Gate is busier – it is the largest export brewery in the world – with its six teams, the place still seems like a mausoleum, or at least a memorial to those thousands who brewed Guinness in the past. No sentimentality here, just plain observation. Yet when I visited the soon-to-be-closed Park Royal brewery, it was reassuring to have to take

Park Royal brewery buildings

my leave of Mike Crawford, the shift supervisor, so that he could go along to his daily 11 a.m. tasting session. Even today, a man stands next to a vat with a cup in his hand. Brilliant.

GIGFY

"Guinness is good for you," or GIGFY as they refer to it at Guinness if they have to, is a phrase that's inscribed on that part of our brain that connects black-and-white beer with a famous name. Yet it's only a bit of advertising that's been handed down to us over the years. To stay on the right side of advertising standards, Guinness hasn't been able to use it since the 1960s. It hasn't appeared on a Guinness poster since 1937. I don't know about you, but that was a long time before

The Dorothy L. Sayers GIGFY Toucan ad

I was born, so how come we know all about it?

The press still loves the story. As recently as November 2003, a piece of scientific research on dogs from the University of Wisconsin proved a pint of Guinness a day taken at mealtimes is good for the heart, whereas a pint of lager does not yield the same benefits. "Although the blood-clotting effects are mainly due to the alcohol, Guinness is full of flavonoids, which help to reduce damage to the lining of the arteries, and are found in dark fruits and berries, red wine and chocolate," said a grateful beagle after one too many lager hangovers.

At the time, a Diageo spokesperson said, "We never make any medical claims for our drinks." Or any claims at all that sound anything like GIGFY. Have those scientists unwittingly stumbled upon Arthur Guinness's great secret? After all, James Joyce did once describe Guinness as "the wine of the country."

Now, advertising is often the first and major way you encounter a brand. It's one thing drinking the beer for yourself, however, and quite another being told what it means. With Guinness, many of us will have GIGFY at the back of our minds without ever knowing why. But largely because of society's current obsession with the responsible drinking message, Guinness goes to inordinate lengths to avoid associating itself with health and well-being, even though the link is hard-wired into the DNA of the brand.

It all goes back to the reason Guinness began advertising in 1929. Guinness was a household name even then, but it felt that if you advertised, it showed the world you had a problem. And Guinness did. Guinness has always been a "guest beer" in UK pubs; unlike other brewers, it had no pub outlets of its own through which to sell its beer. As a quality beer, it relied on its excellent reputation to keep public demand and therefore pub stocks high.

During the 1920s, however, sales slumped badly, like never before. If this trend continued, Guinness would find increasing difficulty in selling its beer to the pub landlords on whom it relied totally, having no pub outlets of its own. But it knew why sales were falling. It had been suffering quality problems for several years. During the First World War, the prime minister, Lloyd George, had passed legislation reducing the alcoholic strength of beer in an attempt to boost the war effort. Guinness was affected more than most brewers because it needed the strength to preserve the quality of its bottled Extra Stout. Without it, the beer would go off easily. People were getting less alcoholic value for their money from a beer they could no longer rely on.

But rely on it a lot of people still did, as Guinness's first advertising agency, S. H. Benson, discovered in 1927. Without any modern market research techniques at their disposal, Benson's directors simply toured Dublin's pubs asking people why they drank Guinness. The reply they invariably received was "Because Guinness is good for you." But Benson's didn't do anything as daft as simply believe what customers told them. They wrote to thousands of UK doctors asking for their comments. And thousands of replies came back assuring them that Guinness was good for just about any ailment

known to humankind. Not only that, but they had been dispensing it for decades.

Consider the times. It was the late 1920s, two decades before the advent of the UK's National Health Service. People had to get their remedies wherever they could, and relied on word of mouth. Advertising hoardings and newspapers were full of ads for potions and lotions and curative

Guinness annual doctors' book, 1963

notions. If fewer people

23

were drinking Guinness, a lot still were because they knew it was good for them. If it wasn't a medicine, it was effectively a tonic.

Guinness was only too happy to rely on the voice of authority figures in the medical profession. Doctors might have been trained scientists, but like the general public they relied on precedent. Where, then, did the doctors get *their* assurance from?

Well, they got it from the doctors of earlier generations, and they got it from... Charles Dickens! There you have it. Who was going to argue with Britain's second-greatest writer? Surely Shakespeare himself would have recommended Guinness had it been brewing when he was alive. And Charles Dickens got his faith in Guinness from an anecdote about one of Wellington's officers. Badly wounded, he called for a pint of Guinness. Not only was he mightily refreshed, but he attributed his recovery to the brew.

If you wanted to know why Guinness was good for you, it was because the Duke of Wellington won the Battle of Waterloo. "Ah, but the Duke of Wellington was Irish!" That's another story. Get on with it.

And get on with it Guinness did. They sent free Guinness to hospitals and to patients who sent in doctors' prescriptions for skin ailments, migraines and other complaints. They used doctors' recommendations as the backbone of their advertising for the next 40 years – long enough for Guinness advertising to become an institution in its own right. And that's why we know about it today. Not because doctors still recommend it for anything; they haven't for 40 years or more.

Even so, you could get Guinness until very recently if you donated blood or were pregnant or recovering from an operation in hospital.

As late as 1961, a Guinness researcher wrote to every doctor in the UK asking for their experience in the therapeutic use of Guinness. Thirty thousand replied, with 11,500 favourable comments and only 83 unfavourable ones (that's just 0.2 percent).

The end of GIGFY

When a UK doctor challenged the "good for you" claim under the Trades Descriptions Act, in the early 1960s, Guinness rolled out what was hardly its most powerful argument. It announced that pigs might help, as they have much the same metabolism as humans. If tests could be done proving that pigs that had had Guinness added to their swill were healthier than those that hadn't, the line would stand. Various companies and research establishments were sounded out, until Guinness finally realized that there were too many variables in pig rearing to be able to substantiate the claim. So Guinness let four decades of heritage slip quietly away, and GIGFY ended with neither a bang nor a whimper, but a grunt.

A PINT OF GUINNESS ADVERTISING

Thanks to years of top-class advertising from the likes of John Gilroy, it's no longer just an in-joke that Guinness advertising is as much a product as Guinness Draught. As it celebrates 75 years of advertising in 2004, Guinness can look back at how things got to be this way – how a successful message that they would now prefer to ignore acted as the foundation stone for all the advertising yet to come. In its effort to get away from GIGFY, Guinness has evolved strategy after strategy, often

Girder Poster (John Gilroy)

confounding the efforts of advertising agencies to execute them creatively.

Slogans that stand out are increasingly hard to come by. It's not just that there are now so many, decades' worth; it was never easy in the first place. Even the great Guinness advertising artist, John Gilroy, had one of his favourite slogans rejected: "Guinness makes loose women tight." Whatever, a good slogan is one that stands the test of time. But times change, which is why Guinness can no longer stand anywhere near "Guinness is good for you," even though the whole world still believes it.

Today, there is very little that Guinness doesn't know about advertising, particularly on TV. Forty or fifty years ago, TV advertising tended to speak down to the viewer, like a

Sea lion poster (John Gilroy)

parent to a child. Today, Guinness understands as well as any brand that it needs a more interactive relationship with today's consumers, taking its brand to wherever they are and encouraging them to enjoy the Guinness experience.

WHEN ADVERTISING IS HISTORY

One sad day soon, because of increasing regulatory activity that seeks to protect people from their own responsibilities, traditional Guinness advertising may disappear for ever. But its spirit will live on through Guinness collectables. Type in the word "Guinness" on the Ebay auction website and your mind will soon be well and truly boggled by the thousands of items for sale from the kaleidoscopic entirety of Guinness advertising history. You'll very quickly come across "The

Guinness Collectables Club – the official site for collectors of Guinntiques." You might find a signed London Irish rugby ball with Guinness logo; a Guinness Extra Cold key ring; a Guinness inflatable beer bucket; a Guinness golfing cap; a Guinness wall clock; a set of 1983 posters; a 1937 original magazine page featuring a "Guinness is good for you" ad... and that's just on the first page.

Many of these collectables started out in life as point-of-sale promotional goods that sales representatives gave publicans as rewards for stocking Guinness. The most famous Guinness creature, the toucan, featured in the widest range of items: waiters' trays, mirrors, menu cards, glass-cloths, large and small models made from Bakelite, fibreglass and pottery, table lamps, wall plaques, water jugs, plates, cruets, badges, engraved glasses, Christmas cards, soft toys... If you think all this is an irrelevant aside, you haven't visited the Guinness Storehouse in Dublin or online. The sheer range of materials that Guinness now sells directly to consumers usually confounds anyone seeing it for the first time.

At Guinness, innovation goes beyond new ways of dispensing the beer; it's also about capturing the image of the brand. With its homeware, clothing, sporting equipment and jewellery, Guinness's James Blackmore collection of the early 1980s may look dated today, but it's a direct precursor of what Guinness currently sells in the Storehouse and at London's Gatwick Airport, and intends to sell on a much wider basis.

Yet there is no point innovating away from the essence of the brand. From its history of providing witty memorabilia to publicans, Guinness has learned exactly what does and doesn't sell in its shops. It's seen how such brands as Harley-Davidson have developed their brand through clothing. By improving quality, Guinness has ensured that people buy these items for themselves, and not just as gifts. On the one hand, Guinness ignores its heritage; on the other, it exploits it to the hilt. This apparent contradiction prompts the question: is there a Guinness experience *without* the Guinness heritage?

STREAM OF IRISHNESS

People enjoy the Guinness experience nowhere more than in its spiritual home of Ireland. Though Guinness is at home in 150 countries around the world, many of which don't know it as an Irish brand, it has only one true spiritual home. There is nowhere like Ireland. Virtually every other pint pulled is a Guinness. Why on earth does the company need to advertise here at all? It didn't until 1959. Ken Tyrrell, Guinness's advertising manager in Ireland in the 1960s, explained it quite simply: "Not only other beers, but all non-essential items such as television sets, washing machines etc. competed with us for the consumer's spending money." [2]

Ireland is a country that has seen its economy develop from a lowly status to first world in a couple of decades, with all the accompanying social tensions. Guinness may be the national drink, but the country is not immune to lager. As early as 1961, Guinness developed its own lager brand, Harp, and saw it become the brand leader within 15 years. By the 1990s, young drinkers were emerging into a world full of fizzy yellow drinks whose advertising promised a more exciting world than that of their forefathers.

The Guinness Storehouse

In Dublin, the Guinness Storehouse is a shining three-year-old example of how Ireland hangs onto the Irishness of its most famous brand. And who can blame it? Guinness is more than a brand in Ireland, it is *the* Irish brand, and one that's been at the heart of the community for 250 years through difficult economic and political times. Meddle with it at your peril.

Today, as we shall explore, Ireland is the DNA of Guinness. Wherever Guinness operates successfully in the world, there's a grain of Irish truth in it. As there is in James Joyce.

THE POWER OF AFRICA

True, there aren't any Irish grains in Nigerian Foreign Extra Stout (they brew it with sorghum instead of barley), but it's Guinness through and through. As it is in Cameroon and Kenya and other African countries that cherish their particular brand of Guinnessness, because it's part of their culture. Guinness has been exporting its oldest brand variant, Foreign Extra Stout, to African shores since 1827. And still today, despite low consumption per head, Africa has the potential to offer Guinness more growth than any other continent in the world.

In many African countries, as in Ireland itself, Guinness is more than just a beer. A beer company could achieve what Guinness has achieved in Africa only by having its roots in communities the length and breadth of the continent. From the way it opened brewery operations in 24 African countries from the early 1960s onward to the way it now supports its HIV-infected workforces throughout Africa with free anti-retroviral drugs for life, Guinness has exemplified how to do things right.

Yet Africa has been a hidden success story, not recognized as such until 2000. Africa has been hidden because the Guinness brand variant sold there has been hidden. Only in the past four years has the impetus of Foreign Extra Stout come to the fore. Until Francis Eames, then a member of the Guinness global brand team, pointed it out, nobody realized that all the growth of the past 40 years had come from FES. Nobody had looked into it. All the focus was on growing Guinness Draught in developed markets (and not with great success by the look of the graph).

Taken separately, the FES markets of Africa, Asia and the Caribbean could look small beer. Taken together, though, they represented 35 percent of the global business. FES had been growing by stealth. Today, it has reached 40 percent, and is still growing and making a huge impact on the whole Guinness brand. Within that story, Africa is the hidden past, yet also the unexplored future. As for the present, we'll leave that to the amazing personality of Guinness's advertising hero in Africa, Michael Power. We'll be seeing far more of the Power later.

DIAGEOGRAPHY

If you're a dedicated corporate Guinness-watcher, you'll have noticed that Guinness is part of a much larger drinks group called Diageo, and that it looks the odd one out in Diageo's brand

Guinness in Ghana

How Guinness got that way

There was something about the 1980s that made respectable market-focused companies stretch into areas they knew nothing about. By the early eighties, Guinness plc, still controlled by the founder's family, had diversified into several unrelated businesses: convenience stores, health farms, hotels and newsagents. Some were making money, others were losing it. Whatever, the eye was definitely not on the beer.

Ernest Saunders was brought in to help turn the company around. And the rest is recrimination and the Guinness family's loss of ownership. Saunders cut costs, selling many of these businesses and buying others. Profits improved in the overheated business climate of the mid-1980s. Saunders still thought it necessary to diversify away from brewing. In 1986, after everything the Guinness family had always said about whisky, he acquired the Scotch whisky distiller Arthur Bell. When this deal was followed swiftly by the hotly contested and ambitious purchase of United Distillers, nothing was ever again the same for the ownership of Guinness. Although Draught Guinness sales roared into life with the arrival of Rutger Hauer as The Man with the Guinness, the beer was never again as important within the Guinness group.

In 1992, the Guinness family finally lost control of the management of the business. In 1998, former board member Jonathan Guinness wrote *Requiem for a family business*. Little wonder that nobody at Guinness wants to talk about Ernest Saunders.

portfolio. You'll know that Guinness contributes around 17 percent of Diageo's profits, but 40 percent of that comes from the secondary brands Guinness owns or distributes, leaving Guinness the beer contributing just over 10 percent of Diageo profits. Guinness is a beer locked firmly into the spirit world.

SPIRITUALIZED

How much say Guinness has in a conglomerate dominated by successful spirits brands such as Smirnoff is a moot point. But the great changes in the world of Guinness have not come about at the hands of Diageo. Since the acquisition of United Distillers 17 years ago, Guinness has contributed less than 20 percent of group profits at the old Guinness group. Diageo has simply inherited the trend.

Back in the early 1990s, things looked very different. Guinness had anticipated the consolidation of the beer industry and looked to be in a position to become a major player in it. But although it bought Desmond & Geddes in Jamaica and has since used it as the basis for a flourishing market in the Caribbean, Guinness also made the disastrous acquisition of Cruz Campo, Spain's largest brewer.

Turning its back on consolidating the beer market had major repercussions for its future direction. It not only retained its spirits brands, including Gordon's Gin and Johnnie Walker, but began negotiations with Grand Metropolitan and all *its* spirits brands about the merged company that in 1997 became Diageo. After some initial uncertainty that saw Guinness merge with United Distillers and Vintners within the group to become Guinness UDV, there came a crunch moment in 2001, when Diageo had to make a decision about its future direction. At that moment, Diageo might have decided to sell its beer brand and focus on spirits, but it decided to stick with Guinness. Since then, things have settled down considerably in the Diageo–Guinness relationship.

Today, the future for Guinness lies with Diageo and with the Diageo way of doing things. And it was from the Diageo way of doing things that Guinness finally acquired its single global brand vision in 2001. All around the world, people see different things in Guinness. But thanks to the "Diageo way of brand building" (fondly known in the organization as "dweeb"), Guinness sees only one big thing in itself: inner strength.

Is Uncle Arthur turning in his grave? Inner strength is certainly something he had. If he was here today he'd be a Diageo man. And he is here. In spirit.

FROM POWER TO STRENGTH

Guinness is a world of moving markets operating at different speeds. In 2000, when Diageo led the huge challenge to unify marketing thinking into one global vision, this was bound to be an issue. After all, the Guinness world is broadly split into two, with draught in the developed world and Foreign Extra Stout in Africa, Asia and the Caribbean.

As it happened, the brand leader, Draught Guinness, was not doing so well, whereas the stealthy underdog, FES, was breaking records by the year. When Guinness banged the two heads together, it came as no surprise that it was the more successful FES that contributed the major element of the new global vision. In a collaborative but laborious process lasting two years, Guinness emerged from its soul-searching with one key brand benefit: Guinness is the global brand of inner strength.

Inner strength
Inner strength is about having the confidence and self-belief to do the things in life we want to do. Inner strength is a highly relevant and motivating concept to men throughout the world who need to believe they're strong, assertive and independent. This is the thinking behind the Guinness global vision from which all marketing initiatives are developed. Guinness brought together its vast heritage and the uniqueness of the brand as it found it in 2000. Inner strength is a powerful positioning that draws on the historical sense of "Guinness is good for you" and "Guinness for strength," as well as the confidence and dynamism associated with more recent ideas such as The Man with the Guinness and Michael Power.

The Guinness Draught markets were attempting to temper the burgeoning physical power of Africa with the more internalized western focus that came of years of sophisticated advertising. Is it working? We'll take a look at that by examining aspects of the first global output of this vision: the "Believe" campaign.

As well as a global key brand benefit, Guinness also developed a global brand essence or set of values that helps its marketers and external agencies to understand and fine-tune their work in the promotion of the brand. "Power," "goodness" and "communion" are the words that define Guinness anywhere and everywhere in the world.

> **Believe**
> In February 2002, "Believe" emerged as Guinness's first-ever global advertising campaign and the earliest expression of the key consumer benefit that "Guinness brings out your inner strength." "Free-in" was an ad created in Ireland and launched in the other Draught markets (the UK, US and Australia). Its message was that Guinness drinkers are discerning individuals who have an inner resolve.

BEYOND GEOGRAPHY

But words are one thing, actions quite another. As a writer, I'm a staunch defender of the power of words. I believe they can underpin our actions, if we mean them. I'm glad to say that Guinness is a brand that means what it says.

A hundred, two hundred years ago, Guinness became a global company largely because it sold its goods into many markets around the world. But that did not make it a global company in the sense we understand today. There are many companies today that have a global network but don't really deserve the label "global brand." With that label come responsibilities that few brands have been able to live up to in word or deed. Why name them here, when there is a far more important brand to talk about: Guinness. A brand that built its global citizenship credentials on going out into the world and brewing its beer in local markets, employing local people, supporting local communities, in places where other companies didn't go or didn't stay.

Is the Guinness brand Irish, British or global, or a mixture of all three? Jon Potter, former Guinness global brand director answers like this: "You can't put this brand into boxes. It depends where you are in the world. The beauty of the brand is that it has different aspects to it. Its values are beyond geography." "Beyond geography" could have been the title of this book, if it hadn't been for the fact that "Guinness is Guinness" is a phrase on so many people's lips.

We started this chapter talking about you and a pint of beer. We've ended it talking about corporate ownership and globalization. If you want to, you can keep it simple and just enjoy the drink. But there's more to this beer than meets the eye. After all, that's what you thought the first time you saw it. That's why you know more about it than you're ready to admit. And there's a whole lot more. My view is that the more you know about Guinness, the more you'll enjoy the beer.

Notes

1   "The greatest invention of the past 40 years is... er, the widget," Chris Murphy, *Daily Mirror*, 10 November 2003.
2   "Guinness Advertising in Ireland," 4 October 1962, internal document from company archive.

Guinness in Malaysia

FORWARD
INNOVATION
& QUALITY

Francis Eames was excited when he burst into the room with an armful of the latest innovations. There's nothing like innovation to bring out the passion in Guinness global brand team managers. Especially when you consider that Guinness has launched three things in the past 50 years, and right now they've got six on the go. Today, Guinness wants to make sure that every innovation carries something of the Guinness DNA to avoid such disasters as Guinness Light from the early 1980s. Among the goodies Francis dropped onto the table were a new bar fount (bar dispenser) for Japan, a new beer for Ghana, a new can for Ireland and a new bottle for Malaysia.

The first thing to catch my eye was the huge Arthur Guinness signature flowing in silver grey up the side of the new Guinness Draught can for Ireland. I'd never seen it writ so large. Why does every can and bottle of Guinness still carry the founder's signature? He's important, yes, but he's been dead for 200 years. Isn't that a little backward for such a forward-looking brand as Guinness?

The truth is that today more than ever, Arthur's name stands for the quality that underpins the Guinness brand, especially in Ireland. As founder, he was the brand's first innovator. And when he innovated, he did so on quality. In his determination to drive his business forward, he refused to look backward, except when it suited his purpose to do so – the essence of Guinness innovation to this very day.

MY GOODNESS, MAGENNIS:
ARTHUR'S FIRST BRANDING ACT

One of the first rules for any new business is to set out your stall well before you begin trading. By the time the first Arthur Guinness came to prominence, there was much gossip in Dublin about this upstart's origins. Was he the descendant of a Cromwellian soldier, or did he emerge from a more acceptable line? One of the more romantic of many stories has it that, to settle any dispute about his ancestry, he appropriated a coat of arms from a well-to-do aristocratic Catholic family called Magennis. Although Arthur was a Protestant by faith, he seems to have got away with it. Indeed, this sleight of hand brought many benefits to Arthur and Guinness over the years. It allowed the family to inherit the title of Earl of Iveagh, which later family members used to

great advantage for the company. It positioned Arthur and Guinness as Protestant business owners with sympathy and understanding for the Catholic cause – very useful!

Arthur would not have recognized the word "innovation," but clearly he knew what it meant: bringing in the new from the old. He also knew that the future of his business

Arthur Guinness

lay in improving the quality of the beer. Today, the company he created still depends on innovation, in the sense of improving the quality of the brand, of which the beer is just a part. Guinness is Guinness... but it's not as black and white as that.

Source: Message left on the "Home" wall of postcards by a visitor to the Guinness Storehouse in Dublin, 28 November 2003

FOREVER BLOWING BUBBLES

What do we recognize as innovation? Well, yes, the widget. But the widget didn't emerge from thin air. It came out of the earlier innovation called Guinness Draught: the beer we've been drinking since 1961. One thing builds on another. Let's follow the line backward for a while.

43

In the 1960s, a Guinness brewer called Tony Carey saw the future when he realized that you could get Draught Guinness in the pub, but you couldn't take it home with you. Unfortunately, nobody was really interested for decades.

Emission impossible
First, they tried to create Draught in bottles with bubbles. That was a 1960s thing. Bottles were what Guinness knew. Bubbles come from air. And cans were a 1970s thing. But after moving the project to cans, Guinness canned the project. The as yet small take-home market did not justify the cost of development. By the streamlined 1980s, a Guinness brewer called Peter Hildebrand had made a breakthrough by creating a jet of foam instead of a jet of air. Guinness was about to start creaming itself.

When falling sales in the recession of the early 1980s was coupled with rising demand for take-home beer, the offspring was commercial pressure: just the right amount to give scientist Alan Forage £5 million to find a solution. After three months of trying to create bubbles in hundreds of ways, Guinness had had a host of failures, but one route with a 5 percent success rate. Not much – but enough to close down other research. In 1985, they perfected and patented the system. In 1986, research confirmed it was a good one. It took two more years to modify the canning machines.

Soon after Draught Guinness In Cans was launched in 1988, it allowed Guinness to become the number 7 take-home brand in Britain, with sales of a million cans a week. It didn't stop people drinking in pubs; draught sales actually grew. The industry copied, but then Guinness invented a new version of the widget for both its cans and bottles (the widget floats at the top instead of sitting at the bottom). It had to; the story of the widget epitomizes Guinness innovation – adapt or die. Now that the off-trade in Britain commands around 35 percent of the market, it won't be long before take-home sales of Guinness overtake those from the pub. Now there's a thought for innovation!

NO DODGING THE DRAUGHT

We take the widget for granted, and we've long accepted Draught Guinness as a fact of life. But the creamy beer we drink today was not widely available until the mid-1960s. A decade later, only half of British pubs stocked it. Before that, people drank Guinness from bottles – the variety you can still buy in supermarkets under the name Guinness Extra Stout. Try some; you'll notice a different flavour and consistency.

With the appearance of keg bitters and lagers in pubs during the 1950s, Guinness had no choice but to develop a draught of its own. Although sales had grown healthily from 2.5 million hectolitres in 1932 to 5.4 million in 1956, they went into sharp decline once the younger generation arrived on the UK scene. It was no coincidence. Younger drinkers did not want to be seen drinking Guinness in bottles when they had new keg bitters and lagers to choose from. Even older drinkers had begun to perceive bottled Extra Stout as the long-life version of the real thing you could get only in Ireland. Here, they'd also had a rudimentary draught system since the 1950s whereby barmen physically injected the pints with special syringes to start the surge.

But as ever with Guinness, things weren't that easy. First, it took the Guinness brewers a long time to recognize the need for a serious solution to draught. They were perfectionists who regarded draught as an adulteration of the real thing: live, unpasteurized beer that fermented in the bottle and conditioned on the shelf. They didn't really care what consumers thought. Second, the technology used to pump the beer from the keg to the fount didn't work with Guinness. The beer was too lively, and, oops, premature ejaculation swiftly followed. If Guinness wasn't to be a bottled beer left on the shelf in a world of draught, the situation called for a different approach.

TAKE YOUR TIME, SON

The problem was solved by an academic mathematician called Michael Ash. He examined all the attempts at dispensing draught that Guinness had made since the 1930s. Some worked, but were too complicated and cumbersome for publicans to use. There was a better solution somewhere. The problem was gas – oh, and Guinness. Other brewers used carbon dioxide to pressurize kegs with no problems, but Guinness? It just couldn't contain itself.

Guinness tried using unpressurized casks, but publicans were only human, and discovered they could add slops back into the Guinness cask. No wonder fewer people were asking for Guinness!

DAFT GUINNESS

Ash's task was to create a pressurized draught Guinness cask that was easy to use and was sealed to prevent tampering. He didn't get much support internally. They called it "Daft Guinness." Between 1956 and 1958, however, Ash and his team developed the Easy Serve system, which pressurized the beer with a mixture of nitrogen and carbon dioxide. But it took until 1963 to iron out the technical problems of having two casks in one, and to wean publicans off a habit that now had explosive consequences. Never mind the objections of older brewers who regarded draught Guinness as a chemical excrescence simply because it had been pasteurized for easier distribution. We would never say that of draught Guinness today, particularly in comparison with all the lagers and beers that are full of artificial additives. Guinness is one of the few beers that can say it's brewed naturally. The dissenting brewers were wrong. The public liked the new Guinness; they found it more palatable, slightly less bitter, and cooler.

Thanks to the persistence of Michael Ash, the guest beer that was about to outstay its welcome soon took its place alongside the nation's favourite draught brews. All for a £20,000 investment. It should have been in the *Guinness Book of Records*.

The *Guinness Book of World Records*

The year 2004 saw the fiftieth anniversary of the *Guinness Book of World Records*. But Guinness didn't celebrate because it no longer owns it. In 2001, it sold the top-selling English book of all time for £45 million to Gullane, owner of Sooty and Thomas the Tank Engine.

Guinness managing director Sir Hugh Beaver had commissioned the book back in 1954, when the British public watched Roger Bannister break the four-minute-mile barrier and became obsessed with athletics records. Bannister's pace-maker, Chris Chataway, had recently joined Guinness and soon persuaded Beaver to publish a slim book full of facts that would settle common pub arguments about who did what and when. Chataway found the McWhirter twins, who ran a small agency offering obscure facts to the press and business, and the first *Guinness Book of World Records* went on sale in 1955.

It was an immediate success. Soon it had to appear in its own pages as the best-selling copyright book of all time. By 2001, Guinness, the global brand of inner strength, no longer regarded a book about achieving world records as core to the brand. Today the book, still under the Guinness name, is sold by Gullane in 77 countries and in 38 languages to a core market of 8- to 13-year-old boys.

Without Ash's innovation, we'd be drinking a very different pint of Guinness today. Or more likely, none at all. We can take a lot for granted. But in the world of Guinness, brewers and marketers have had to fight (sometimes among themselves) for over 200 years to take the brand forward from one stage of its existence to the next.

THE BATTLE FOR THE BRAND

Many people, including some who write about Guinness today and should know better, think of Guinness only in terms of Great Britain and Ireland. Yet Guinness has fought a two-century-long battle to take its beer beyond its spiritual homeland and out into the world. It has been a battle for the very brand itself, and it has depended on ten innovative step changes:

STEP 1: MAKE ONE THING WELL

Arthur Guinness began by brewing several beers and ales at St James's Gate Brewery in Dublin. On a trip to London, he saw porters enjoying a mixture of beers and ales named after them. When porter was imported to Dublin, Arthur decided that the only way to succeed in business was to brew a better porter and beat the English at their own game. It took him decades, but when the beer was established, he abandoned the other ales he had brewed in order to focus on the quality of one.

STEP 2: EXTEND THE MARKET

To grow his business, Arthur had to go beyond the limited Irish market, where few people had the money to buy his beer except in ports such as Cork and Belfast. The idea was to sell the porter back to the English and around the world.

Extending the market was one thing. But from 1769, when six and a half barrels of Guinness left the port of Dublin on a sailing ship bound for England, the big issue for Guinness was how to make the porter travel better.

Hogs' heads and ships' bottoms

It was the early nineteenth century, less than a hundred years after the fictional seafaring exploits of Robinson Crusoe had fired the imagination and fed the desire for adventure on the high seas. Sailing vessels were much the same and sailing conditions scarcely less treacherous. The brew called Guinness Foreign Extra Stout that's famous in Africa and Asia today was first recorded in ledgers as West Indies Porter as early as 1802. Early records show Barbados, Trinidad, Demerara and Jamaica as recipients of anything from 10 to 37 hogsheads (1 hogshead = 52 gallons or 416 pints). As British influence expanded throughout the world, so Guinness followed, exporting to the US, Australia and South Africa. Small beginnings, but beginnings none the less.

STEP 3: OUTSOURCE THE REST

Up to 1830, when shipments were fairly small, Guinness supplied customers directly from St James's Gate. The more Guinness was exported, however, the greater the task of managing the quality between the brewer and the consumer. Any number of factors, from exposure to sunlight to extreme cold, could render the beer unreliable, acid, flat, stale, full of sediment and undrinkable. It all made the exportation of Guinness slow and expensive.

For brewers quick on the uptake like Guinness, the recipe for greater profits from the overseas trade lay in just brewing the beer and sending it to independent agencies. From 1830, agencies in London, Liverpool and Bristol took over bottling and distribution. They bottled, stored, shipped, warehoused and advertised in their own markets.

It was the power and sheer drive of these independent bottling companies that helped to take Guinness exports around the world in the nineteenth century. By 1884, St James's Gate had become the largest brewery in the world. Exports represented only about 5 percent of sales, but the brewery's fame was spreading across the globe.

This was effectively handing over quality and innovation to other companies. Was it a good strategy? It was the way that non-bottling brewers like Guinness came to dominate the overseas trade, in terms of seeing their beer exported all over the world. But it wasn't Guinness itself that developed its trade, but Read's, Burke's, Porter's and their ilk. It was only a matter of time before Guinness and other brewers began to ask: "Who owns our brand?"

Busy little bottlers

The small merchant bottlers were the brave enterprises opening and developing the markets, taking the risks and controlling the trade. Their sole purpose was to scramble among themselves for the contracts of brewers like Guinness and Bass, then deliver their brews and beverages to far-flung corners of the world under their own brand names.

Where Guinness was concerned, as long as the business was FOB – free on board at Dublin – then it didn't matter where it went or who drank it.

STEP 4: BRAND YOUR PRODUCT

In the nineteenth century, the main way for a beer to distinguish itself from its rivals was by the picture on the label. Pictures, designs and especially "brands" featuring animals, birds and other familiar images were also used. To protect a company's exclusive right to use such designs, a trademark registry was set up in London in the 1860s. Among brewers, Bass was the first company to use and register a distinctive mark: the Bass triangle. Guinness soon followed by registering its harp design and trademark label. When the bottlers followed suit, protecting their right to use whatever names they chose to sell Guinness wherever they wanted, the battle of the brand truly began.

Nevertheless, the relationship between Guinness and bottler remained a symbiotic one. Each needed the other. But in truth, the bottlers were the brand. Tensions inevitably arose, as they could incur severe losses. The protracted fermentation process of FES caused problems even for the most experienced bottlers. Unsatisfactory beer couldn't be returned to the brewery in those days, making compensation claims hard to substantiate. Guinness wouldn't pay up, so the bottlers had to.

The better and more experienced bottlers tended to survive. Although this was probably better for Guinness in terms of quality, these survivors had largely outdone their competitors by advertising their names on the label loudly and proudly, and larger than "Guinness." Doing so not only made it easy for imitators but led to the bottlers being perceived as the brand. This was not at all good for Guinness. After all these

Everyone else's Guinness stout

years, it had a better-quality beer that came from the largest brewery in the world. On the other hand, there were so many "named" bottlers and imitators that the Guinness brand was in danger of sinking beneath a sea of labels.

A sea of labels
Burke registered its Cat trademark in 1876. T. B. Hall marketed Guinness under the Boar's Head label. T. P. Griffin registered the Griffin trademark. Macfee of Liverpool was selling Guinness under the Lightship brand in Egypt as late as 1921, and Australia as late as 1925. J. P. O'Brien had different brands for Guinness in different markets: Dagger, Tribute, Jack of Hearts, Prize Medal, Target. Robert Porter sold the well-known Bull Dog brand, which still survived until recently on Guinness FES neck labels in Malaysia. W. E. Johnson sold Guinness under the Donkey and Compass brands in Brazil and other parts of South America. Blood Wolfe used its Z trademark in conjunction with the Guinness label. There were numerous others. It was all Guinness. And some of it wasn't Guinness that said it was.

STEP 5: EDUCATE THE CUSTOMER

In the 1890s, Guinness decided to get stuck into the overseas trade and start laying down the law. It didn't know who drank its beer. Its customers were the export bottlers. Now Guinness stopped behaving like a supplier and assumed rightful control of its brand in a way that befitted the biggest brewer in the world.

First, it imposed its Guinness trademark label on the entire FES trade, with rigorous conditions. This was a defining moment for global brand dominance. Bottlers on whom Guinness depended were told to discontinue other stouts and bottle nothing but Guinness. They were allowed to continue using their own well-established brand names as long as they bottled no other stout and gave due prominence to the Guinness name and trademark on their labels.

The bottlers naturally resented it. After all, it wasn't Guinness that paid compensation to retail outlets when the beer went off. It wasn't Guinness that fought the forgers and paid the legal bills. To cover themselves, the bottlers simply put up their prices and made Guinness even more uncompetitive in a tough marketplace.

But the battle with the bottlers had just begun. When you hand over your brand (for what seems like a good reason at the time) and allow somebody else to develop it successfully for over 50 years, they're not going to give it back without a fight.

Burke's Guinness label

The battle with Burke's

The fiercest battle was with Burke's, Guinness's largest customer. Between 1900 and 1905, Guinness had to take Burke's to task several times over its use of objectionable labels and advertisements. Burke's even registered the label "Burke's Bottled Guinness Stout" in the US. Faced with the astonishing possibility that Guinness was about to take its biggest customer to court for fraudulent description, Burke's caved in. Its new label proclaimed "Guinness Stout Bottled by Burke's." Guinness had taken back control of its brand.

STEP 6: SEND IN THE CAVALRY

Forgeries were big trouble. In 1889, when news came that there was widespread forgery of the trademark label in the US, as well as counterfeiting and adulteration of FES, Guinness had to sit up and take notice. Anyone could sell Guinness anywhere at whatever price they chose, both wholesale and retail. Inferior local products were cleaning up. But *were* they inferior? Guinness knew nothing about the condition of its beer once it had left the Dublin brewery. This state of affairs could not continue. It was damaging the brand and its reputation at a time when competition was growing from Europe, and especially from German lager. It was time to send in the cavalry.

But it took years to find the right man. In 1898, Guinness appointed Arthur T. Shand as its first global salesman.

As imported beers such as FES had become uncompetitive in the US market, Shand pressed the Guinness board to persuade export bottlers to slash their prices. He also recommended bottling in the US to reduce costs. In 1910, as a result of his efforts, Burke's became the first export bottler to bottle overseas, in New York. In 1912, the year the *Titanic* sank with

Shand stand
Arthur T. Shand had the tough job of Guinness world traveller. He had to find answers to some pressing questions. Who was drinking FES and what was it like when it reached them? Was the name Guinness prominent on labels? Who were the imitators? Where were the trademark problems? Who were the fraudsters? From the moment Shand embarked on his travels in the US and Canada, Guinness began suing left, right and centre. Although this was time-consuming and costly, it worked: American sales rose by 33 percent between 1900 and 1904.

Guinness in the hold, Seigal Cooper, the world's largest grocery firm, began bottling Guinness in the US. By 1913, there were six bottlers in New York. By 1914, hundreds of specialist bottlers in the UK had been whittled down to around 30, all competing head to head for sales in worldwide markets.

STEP 7: SEND IN THE EXPERT

Shand spent much of the first decade of the twentieth century trying to persuade the Guinness board to let him introduce Extra Stout on draught into saloons in New York. But by 1912, not only had the draught not taken off, but it was actually in decline. Shand did not understand why.

Guinness suspected it had something to do with the quality of the beer. The company sent over one of its scientific brewers to find out. Ben Newbold was living proof of the Guinness commitment to quality. He spent two months touring the US with Shand in early 1913. Not only did he get to the bottom of the Extra Stout on draught problem, he succeeded in making the whole Guinness approach more systematic, scientific and innovative.

Newbold worked out that by the time the Guinness reached saloons, it had undergone a series of temperature changes that greatly reduced its quality. Handling by the shippers and the export bottlers left a lot to be desired. How could the stout be kept cool in transit on the White Star liners? It would often be left boiling in the sun on the quayside when offloaded. Newbold recommended ways of keeping beer fermenting in casks cool both in cargo holds and on arrival prior to bottling.

STEP 8: UNDERSTAND YOUR CUSTOMERS

If you know what your customers like and how they use your product, you're in a good position to meet their needs. Newbold was one of the first market researchers of his day. He asked simple but important questions: who drinks Guinness in the States, and why? But unlike salesman Shand, he could use his technical background to draw the right

Source: Message left on the "Home" wall of postcards by a visitor to the Guinness Storehouse in Dublin, 28 November 2003

conclusions. In 1913 he saw that Guinness was still being drunk primarily as a tonic rather than a beverage. It wasn't surprising. Doctors recommended it and ads reinforced it: "The world's most nourishing tonic – Recommended for invalids."

Shand had persuaded bottlers to adapt to drinker behaviour by producing half-pint bottles so that the contents wouldn't go flat. But Newbold went further. He said that Guinness would suit the American taste better if it was sold as "young" and palatable as possible. This would also help to swing its image from a medicine to a beverage, so boosting sales. It's an argument that still stands today.

STEP 9: BOTTLE YOUR BUSINESS

The First World War had disastrous consequences for Guinness's overseas trade. Then came Prohibition in America, which lasted until 1933. The loss of the American market affected not just Guinness but also the export bottlers in the UK. There were too many of them – 18 – trying to make a profit out of too small a trade.

Guinness took the bull by the horns. In 1932, it bought a small bottler, Alexander Macfee of Liverpool. After 100 years, Guinness was investing in a bottler for the first time. Macfee absorbed many of the unviable smaller bottlers and did a great deal of work on improving the storage and cooling of FES in transit on board ship.

In 1935, Guinness persuaded the three main bottlers – Read, Burke and Porter – to amalgamate as Export Bottlers Ltd. Smaller bottlers either joined this or Macfee, or went out of business. The new arrangement soon succeeded in overseas markets: the bottlers were working more efficiently and in a common cause; transit conditions had been improved. Then World War II struck, and jettisoned all the progress once again.

Completing the bottler strategy took twenty years, but it acted as the springboard to the creation of a global brand. In 1950, Macfee changed its name to Guinness Exports and took over Export Bottlers. For the first time, Guinness was in control of its entire export business and was able to expand into new markets around the world in a structured way. But this still meant exporting to overseas markets under the brand names of the small bottling companies it had taken over. These brands were consumers' way of recognizing the product in

Guinness Exports Ltd

widely varying markets. Even today, the Wolf's Head brand formerly owned by Blood Wolfe is so well known in Indonesia, Thailand and Singapore that people still ask for it by name.

In 1950, FES sales had fallen to 35,000 barrels a year. By 1960, Guinness was exporting more than 300,000 barrels a year from Liverpool to the rest of the world.

Guinness Exports Ltd

STEP 10: EXPORT THE ESSENCE

After two centuries of getting out into the world, solving all the problems of quality and shipping and finally establishing its own successful export business, Guinness decided that it would be better to brew overseas after all. It had done things the hard way: making beer at home and exporting it around the world. But beer consists mainly of water, which is heavy and bulky to transport. Bulky foreign imports attract massive import duties. Beer itself is volatile and best drunk fresh. The best way to control costs and make a better beer was to brew it in the markets themselves.

Guinness decided to open two overseas breweries in Nigeria and Malaysia, top markets for Foreign Extra Stout. It could bear the costs and handle local political considerations. It would be in charge of brewing. Quality Guinness was assured.

But if it was to grow its other overseas markets, it would have to brew Guinness under licence with local brewers. It wasn't just a question of sharing the profits. When you have a great product and you hand it over to other people to make, you wonder if it is going to retain anything about it that makes it great. As Arthur knew at the very beginning, if you don't make a quality beer you aren't going anywhere. After 200 years, Guinness was faced with the same problem.

The difficulty was that most overseas brewers made lager. Only ale brewers could brew Guinness, but they were few and far between. It seemed the only way Guinness could get into most of these markets was to brew Guinness in lager breweries. But how? You couldn't make stout in a lager brewery; it used a different process. Guinness decided to develop a concentrated essence of FES that could be dropped into a basic brew of white beer or lager. This would solve the cost, quality and production difficulties at one fell swoop.

It took the whole of the 1960s to perfect the blend of the extract. Now that the exact flavour of Dublin FES could be reproduced anywhere in the world, consistency could be achieved in both brand and product. Using the concentrate allowed Guinness to make a profit in markets where it didn't have breweries, and overcame the problem of import duties at the same time. Globalization became effective. By 1974, 13 licensed breweries were using the concentrate. At first, it was known as Concentrated Mature Beer. Today, it's called Guinness Flavour Extract and is still the basis for brewing Guinness under licence in hundreds of breweries overseas.

Phew! Who said a brand is just about its logo?

DRAUGHT AND FOREIGN EXTRA STOUT: THE TWO WORLDS OF GUINNESS

In the 1950s, the Guinness world consisted of Guinness Foreign Extra Stout (soon to have an exciting future based on overseas breweries) and Guinness Extra Stout (which was bottled and had a limited future in a world of keg draught beer). But Michael Ash's invention of the draught-dispensing Easy Serve cask for top Guinness markets in Ireland and Great

Britain meant that the brand tended to focus mainly on the draught markets for the next 40 years. Here was the first new Guinness variant for over 150 years. And Foreign Extra Stout, which was still much the same as when first recorded in 1802, was allowed to grow and develop almost unnoticed. All the innovations of the previous 200 years had pointed toward the creation of a single global brand, but Guinness existed in two separate worlds.

ASIA HAS THE BOTTLE

No brand can afford to take any aspect of its development for granted. The prospects for Foreign Extra Stout in Guinness's African and Asian markets looked outstanding. Yet although it had established a brewery in Malaysia and set up licensing agreements all around Asia during the 1960s and 1970s, Guinness closed its eyes to FES in the region. It ended up taking the whole of Asia for granted in the last two decades of the twentieth century. Even as late as the 1990s, most of Guinness's focus was still on Great Britain and Ireland. It never really appreciated what FES contributed to the business, or noticed that it was constantly growing in all its markets in Asia, Africa and the Caribbean.

FROM RICKSHAW TO ROLEX

The Asian world in which FES is sold is changing everywhere. Malaysia and Singapore have become industrial economies. By the time Guinness people started looking at this phenomenal growth, Asia's boom had come and gone. But it still delivered the money. In the fast-growing economies where overall beer sales grew, Guinness lost share but held volume. Gradually, however, the markets grew away from Guinness.

Until the 1990s, Guinness had much to be proud of in Asia. It had been there for a century. The second overseas brewery was built in Malaysia in the early 1960s, and Guinness introduced its African business model to the region. By the 1980s, Guinness was market leader in Malaysia, with 40 percent of the beer market. Similar growth was happening throughout the region.

But by the mid-1980s, Asia had jumped out of the economic category that fitted Guinness's African business model. Its countries were no longer less developed, but newly industrializing. Guinness hadn't moved with them, partly because it still had a big base of drinkers. But these drinkers were less and less at the forefront of these newer societies. Guinness gradually became marginalized, especially in Malaysia and Singapore, its largest markets. In China, it was stuck in the traditional market of shorts and a handcart, whereas the big growth

Ouch, it bites!

In 1998, the Asian tiger crept up and bit Guinness where it hurts. It was hardly surprising. Having nurtured Asia so well during the 1960s and 1970s, Guinness had ignored its growing years, and now it was too late. The market had crashed.

Asia has always been important to Guinness in financial terms. Beer prices in Asia are very high. In 1995/96, Asia contributed 25 percent of the entire global Guinness profit from only 12 percent of the sales volume. Profits are harder for Guinness to come by than in other overseas markets, as most of its business takes the form of joint ventures with local concerns. Guinness soon discovered that turning its back on the tiger for nearly 20 years had been a terrible mistake.

was coming from the educated, sophisticated, wealthy white-collar market, which had moved on to mobile phones and higher brand aspirations. Guinness was part of their parents' outlook. It took Guinness a long time to realize how much it had lost in Asia.

LAGER, LAGER, BURNING BRIGHT

Guinness should have seen lager coming. It had always been big in Asia. German brewers flourished in Singapore before the Second World War. Heineken took over. Guinness built both the Singapore and Malaysia beer markets before Carlsberg came along in the mid-1960s. When Guinness merged with Asian brewer Anchor in 1980, the market was split 50/50 with Carlsberg. Lager commanded a bigger proportion of the market, but Guinness did not develop as an alternative. Instead, the lager brands in the Guinness Anchor portfolio were promoted to compete.

During the 1990s, another step change took place in the market while Guinness was looking the other way. Tiger Beer emerged as the new icon in Asian markets, ousting Guinness Anchor and Carlsberg to become the biggest lager brand. There had been a big shift in attitudes; for aspiring Asians, Tiger had become the brand to be seen drinking. It was as good as any international beer, but from the region. Although Guinness was regarded as local too, it was dated; the previous generation's beer.

Ironically, it's taking a bottle to turn things around in Asia – the very one Francis Eames brought excitedly into the room at the beginning of this chapter. We'll let him explain: "The original bottle had been around for a hundred years and wasn't very individual or adventurous. It was living on past glories." True enough, it was the contents and not the packaging that made Guinness stand out in markets like Asia.

The wrong kind of curry
The Guinness brand strategy in Asia in the 1990s has been described as "pins on maps." The idea was to find new markets for Guinness and cover the world. A major push in 1993/94 to extend Guinness from its British Empire base into East Asia came too late. The 1998 economic crisis had been looming for years. Besides, Guinness had brewed in Thailand for 20 years without ever making much of the Thai market. It opened a licensed brewery in Vietnam with a French brewer. Similar ventures took place in Cambodia, Sri Lanka, China and Nepal. There were import arrangements in Laos and the Philippines. Cambodia and Sri Lanka worked well for a while, but difficulties with local partners closed them down. FES had always gone well with the spicy food markets, but the green curry tastes of Thailand and Vietnam didn't seem to suit it at all.

So in the summer of 2003, Guinness introduced a new bottle shape into Malaysia, Singapore and Hong Kong, its three largest markets. It's sleek, elegant, modern and unlike anything else on the shelves. Guinness hopes it will appeal to younger drinkers, and is marketing it as a hand-held bottle in an attempt to popularize the brand in bars and other entertainment venues where people drink straight from the bottle.

Guinness is Guinness, and a bottle is just a bottle. On their own, cosmetic changes never really arouse consumers' interest. For the bottle launch in Singapore, Saatchi & Saatchi produced a campaign encouraging people to think about bottle shapes and vote on a series featured in ads. One design showed a macho bottle based on Thor; others included a moon, a guitar and a bull's horn. The copy ran, "For a change, here's a bottle that's actually shaped like a bottle. No mythical gods. No grinning moons. No bulls. And no strange looks from people at the bar either."

In Malaysia, the new bottle is already boosting sales. Adorers are delighted the shape has changed; *they'd* changed in the past 20 years, so why hadn't Guinness? The new bottle is the first real initiative to revitalize the Guinness brand in Asia since before the tiger was a glint in its roaming father's eye.

What can a bottle achieve? Probably more than advertising can. In Asia, advertising is often limited to what you can do in store at the point of sale. There, the bottle can be seen and appreciated for its very different, sophisticated, modern design. There are no TV ads in Islamic Malaysia, the biggest Guinness market. In Indonesia, which is also Muslim, but of a more secular kind, there is no advertising at all.

> **Man of the year**
> Even so, Asian advertising can be successful, as the more sophisticated markets of Malaysia, Singapore and Hong Kong have shown with Adam King, a development of the Michael Power persona from Africa. King's latest campaign, "Someone's going to do it, why not you?" features aspirational scenarios – "Be man of the year," "Be a millionaire," "Write a bestseller," "Be a talkshow host" – that suggest people can be anyone they want to be, if only they believe in themselves.

NO TIME LIKE TODAY

When the Asian crisis hit, attention moved to Diageo's more successful spirits brands in Asia. The spotlight was on Johnnie Walker, not Guinness. It seemed Asia's time had come and gone. But it hadn't. The innovation was a long time in development, but Guinness has something new to show that it's moved on.

The story of the FES bottle is that if you want to go forward, you can't ignore the past. You just have to put it behind you. Guinness has seen huge potential for growth, and the new bottle is something to build on once again. Move on, but keep what you've got. And grow. Even in Indonesia. *Especially* in Indonesia.

Guinness drinkers in Indonesia, unlike those in Malaysia and Singapore, are blue-collar and mostly rural. Their GDP per capita is only US$500, compared to US$20,000 in Singapore. To them, the Guinness brand today still represents long-held notions of physical power and strength. It's a huge, mostly Muslim market, the world's fourth largest population. Even if only a small percentage drink Guinness, that's an awful lot of drinkers.

The brand lessons from Asia are these: be very careful who you team up with and never ever take your eye off the ball. And it's never too late to innovate. If any part of the Guinness world is crying out for innovation, it's Asia. And now it's got the bottle.

IN THE JAPANESE THEATRE

"Fail. Fail again. Fail better." So said Samuel Beckett, Irish playwright and man of letters. And this theatrical message is one that could well be applied to Guinness's approach to innovation in Japan. In this sophisticated beer market, Guinness's joint venture with Sapporo, one of the nation's largest brewers, had made little headway.

Japan is unusual in Asia for being a Guinness Draught market. There was absolutely no progress until Guinness put a new bar fount into research. All of a sudden, the possibility of developing a draught business in Japan became the focus of the entire market in Asia. Could the company move its business from a mere 500 bars to 50,000? How did Guinness manage to get into this position? It was all down to a much-derided experiment that took place in the UK in 2002.

In August 2002, Guinness trialled FastPour – a dispensing system that scraps the two-part pour and delivers a pint in 25 seconds – in 35 pubs in London and Yorkshire. According to Jon Potter, Guinness's global brand director, "It was just an experiment. We wanted to see whether 119.5 seconds was equity or a barrier. It was well worth our while testing this. We found that the need for FastPour isn't that great. There is no barrier. The two-part pour *is* our equity. Sometimes, occasion demands that people switch out of Guinness. The FastPour experiment was an excellent example of rigour in the innovation process."

And so it was. Even though traditionalists saw it differently, including the Campaign for Real Ale (CAMRA), which accused Guinness of encouraging a rush-rush society. And rival Murphy's announced it was introducing its own Fastflow dispensing system before Guinness had even announced the results of its trial. But Murphy's doesn't have the brand equity of Guinness. Besides, some inspired thinking saw to it that the FastPour technology, which uses ultrasound to release the nitrogen and carbon dioxide needed to create the characteristic surge and creamy head, was soon put to much better use elsewhere in the Guinness world. In Japan.

WAIT FOR IT

In February 2004, Guinness launched a system in Japan that uses ultrasound to initiate the beer from bottles rather than kegs. Having discovered that its brand equity is based on all good things coming to those who wait, why would Guinness want to do this in Japan, a developed beer market?

Surge and see
How does it work? You place a glass on the beer unit of the fount. You open a bottle of Guinness made especially for this process, and pour it into the glass. With no widget inside the bottle, the beer is flat. You switch the unit on. After an ultrasound pulse lasting a second and a half, the surge starts. The glass comes off the fount and is served to you, with full creamy head.

The important factor here is that it's not about the wait. It's about perceptions surrounding the quality and freshness of the beer. In Japan, that's how you get new recruits. The beer will be fresher if more people drink it. So how do you get more people to drink it?

TAKE IT TO THEIR HEARTS

Anybody who has researched the Japanese consumer market knows how its people love a sense of theatre. Guinness created a simple lighting effect for the fount. Unlike most beer founts, where the beer glass is below the counter, this one is above the counter in full view, and lit up to special effect. In research, it went down a storm. It tripled the sales of Guinness in outlets that already had Draught, and was an eye-opener for bars that couldn't have Draught because they lacked the space for keg units. So bar owners could look at it from the point of view of convenience as well as new custom.

Perhaps the true innovation, though, lay in the recognition that service is at table for half the Japanese beer-drinking public. As these customers wouldn't get the effect of the lit-up surging fount at the bar, the simple answer was to bring the fount to their table, where it clips on and drinkers can serve themselves. Magic, with lights attached!

But the real prize for Guinness is that it can rip out keg units in places where it currently sell little Guinness, and get into thousands of outlets where it has never been before. All to deliver a fresher pint of Guinness in a more appealing way. Sounds like a win–win situation to me.

THE NEW BABY

Thanks to its dynamic approach to innovation, Guinness is getting used to winning situations. Now a new child has joined the family. It's the newest kind of Guinness since Guinness Draught in 1961, and it's Africans who are drinking it.

Guinness Extra Smooth was launched in Ghana in July 2003. It's a nitrogenated smoother-drinking form of Guinness Foreign Extra Stout, 2 percent lower in alcohol at 5.5 percent. There's no widget involved; instead, a little added nitrogen is released when you open the bottle. You don't get the full creamy surge, but it's a step toward it. At 500 ml, the bottle is bigger than FES at 300 ml, and much closer to lager size.

Extra Smooth is a response to the discovery that people weren't drinking FES when they were out with their mates. FES was perceived as too strong for a session, and besides it's quite expensive for African drinkers. Extra Smooth is easier to drink than carbonated beer, and cheaper than FES. But isn't that a bit of a risk for Guinness?

Well, Extra Smooth is also a response to the Castlemilk Stout introduced by S. A. Breweries in Ghana two years earlier. Castlemilk took 25 percent of a beer market that had been 75 percent lager and 25 percent Guinness FES. Interestingly, it took its quarter share entirely from lager. It was lower in alcohol than FES, and marketed like lager, yet it had stout values. It was time for Guinness to defend its position. It was also a great opportunity. The only risk was whether a new Guinness variant would eat into its own FES volume share.

Guinness took the risk. Guinness Extra Smooth immediately began eating into Castlemilk's share, leaving FES intact. To say that Guinness Africa is excited about the possibilities for Extra Smooth in tandem with FES is something of an understatement.

FRESH FRESH FRESH

Despite the recent decade-long attack of the hiccups, Uncle Arthur also has cause to be excited about developments in his brand's spiritual home. When Guinness put his name on a can more prominently than ever before in October 2003, it did so to make a statement about the growing importance of the Irish take-home or off trade. In Ireland, there is no rejection of Guinness as a beer, but there is a rejection of the environment in which it is sometimes served. Younger people have turned to trendier, fast-turnover bars that don't provide the right occasion to serve Guinness in the way it should be served.

But how could Guinness persuade consumers that Guinness Draught In Cans is actually as good as in pubs when they know the company has never taken it seriously?

Answer 1: Improve the quality of the product and make a big splash about it. The beer is pasteurized in a slightly different way, and the same volume goes into a smaller can. It's that widget again, you see. It used to demand 60 ml of head space in a can. Trouble was, although that head space got flushed with nitrogen, you couldn't exclude all the oxygen, which meant the beer could go off more quickly than you'd like. So Guinness has reduced the head space to 30 ml, which effectively reduces oxidization by 80 percent. The beer will taste better for longer. Talk about new and improved! Guinness Ireland has launched its first-ever ad to celebrate the home-drinking experience. In Ireland, that's quite a revolution.

Answer 2: Rugby. Guinness Draught In Cans now sponsors the Irish rugby team. It's another huge signal about the value Guinness places on this format. It wants people to understand that it's a better liquid than before: better when fresh, better when three weeks old, better when six months old.

And what about the packaging? Arthur is bigger; the harp logo seems larger. The golden holding bar beneath it is now curved, creating a greater sense of immediacy. Perhaps the greatest innovation is the silver tone that features at the bottom, gradually merging into black and adding a lightness to this very sleek can. According to Guinness Ireland brand controller Mark Ody, "It's supposed to say 'freshness'." Uh oh! I can feel that question coming on that everybody wants to ask. "Does the beer taste better in Dublin than anywhere else?" And the Guinness answer? Mark Ody again: "The myth of the beer tasting better in Dublin comes from the truth that a pint in Dublin might not be a week old. In England, it can be two months in the chain. It goes to the depot, then to the wholesaler, and so on. It's pure myth and speculation. But fresh is fresh is fresh."

Personally, I think you have to be a regular Guinness drinker to answer that question. How do you know whether a beer tastes better in one place than another if you don't drink it regularly? Most people who visit Dublin don't. Yet when they visit, they buy Ireland, and tune their tastebuds accordingly.

At the end of his demonstration session, Francis Eames handed me three of the new Guinness Draught In Cans from Ireland. I'd soon be testing the quality for myself, and agreeing with Francis, who said: "Guinness has only scratched the surface in most of its markets. It's about finding the right kinds of Guinness for the right occasions in the right countries. There's no point in having me-too stuff. Every innovation has to really satisfy a need that isn't being satisfied. Every innovation has to be astonishing."

Arthur would have been proud, but surprised. For it is truly astonishing that the issue he faced when he first tried to extend his business at the end of the eighteenth century is the very one faced by Guinness in its home market at the beginning of the twenty-first. Some things don't change. Guinness has to be fresh: fresh to the taste and fresh to the eye. And sometimes that takes a little persuasion.

Watch this space
The next Guinness innovation will change the way we drink and how we drink. It will make the widget seem like an invention from a bygone age. I know all about it, and I can't tell.

OUTWARD
ADVERTISING

I travelled a long way to meet Rutger Hauer. A journey of 50 million miles over 17 years. But when I got to Mars I found he'd moved house. So what he said in that very first Man with the Guinness commercial in 1987 was true.

Life on Mars
The very first Man with the Guinness ad in 1987 featured a surreal backdrop with Rutger Hauer talking directly to camera: "The planet Mars is paradise. Voices are never raised in argument. Never. There's only one sex. So no emotional problems. No fast cars. No noisy discos. Everyone is equal and lives to 803. Me? I sold up and moved to Earth."

Rutger Hauer was the best thing to happen to Guinness since the invention of Guinness Draught. Before he came along, 66 percent of Guinness drinkers were over 35, and the brand was slowly disappearing with its older customers. After he came along, 66 percent of Guinness drinkers were under 35, and the overall amount of Guinness drunk was way, way higher. He rescued Guinness from its flat-capped working-class image and made it into a sophisticated modern brand for the late 1980s.

If it hadn't been for him, this book wouldn't have been written. He converted a lager drinker into a Guinness Adorer. I was 28 years old and fed up with chemical hangovers induced by fizzy yellow disco juice. When Rutger Hauer appeared on my television screen, I experienced an epiphany, moved quietly on from Paul Hogan and fell in love with The Man with the Guinness. Sure I was ripe for it, but it was the advertising that did it. And that advertising was pure genius.

And Guinness is Guinness... but it's not as black and white as that.

The Man with the Guinness

For critics, he was a sort of manic Luftwaffe flying instructor. For Guinness Adorers, he was an otherworldly individual with a charisma and power all his own. For the brand, he was a walking talking pint of Guinness. If you bought into Rutger, you knew you were not just one of the crowd when you drank a pint of Guinness. You were a free spirit, intelligent, able to make your own choices. The MWTG ads enabled you to feel that way from 1987 to 1994. To some he spoke gibberish. To others, he uttered the truths of the soul. "It's not easy being a dolphin."

PEOPLE LOVE GUINNESS ADVERTISING

Advertising. We all love advertising, especially if it reminds us of the past. The British public loved Gilroy's Guinness animals during their heyday in the 1930s, 1940s and 1950s. They loved it when Guinness reintroduced Gilroy's toucan in 1979, and complained bitterly when it was dropped for good in 1982. They also loved the "Guinnless" campaign that followed, because it was clever enough to borrow some of the imagery from Gilroy's posters of the 1930s. People love Guinness advertising.

Gilroy is good for Guinness

John Gilroy was 32 when he produced his first ad for Guinness in 1930. He'd been an in-house artist with Benson's, Guinness's advertising agency, since 1925. Unusually, he combined remarkable talents for design and writing. His first big campaign was "Guinness for strength." The man with the girder was in fact the very first man with the Guinness.

By 1935, he was producing Guinness animals such as the sea lion, toucan and ostrich for his "My goodness, my Guinness" posters. "I have always been a jolly man and I thought the Guinness campaign needed a touch of humour," he said. His famous "Dig for victory" posters boosted morale during the Second World War. Gilroy worked on Guinness projects into the 1960s, producing more than a hundred posters and advertisements over 35 years. He turned down a lucrative job writing for Disney in Hollywood. David Ogilvy said Gilroy's posters "made Guinness part of the warp and woof of English life, and have never been excelled – anywhere."

Gilroy's Guinness animals. The Guinness Harp (Jan–Feb 1959)

Source: Message left on the "Home" wall of postcards by a visitor
to the Guinness Storehouse in Dublin, 28 November 2003

One writer said that Guinness has been more imaginatively,
elegantly and persuasively advertised than any other product.
Others have called it *the* advertising icon in Britain, "arguably
the brand of the century"[1] and "a logo in a glass."[2] How do we
get to the heart of this genius? We could start by defining what
we mean by genius. I'm with George Steiner on this. Genius is
not originality, but the capacity to make and regenerate myths
and parables for a modern audience. And that's how I judge
Guinness advertising.

February 7, 2004 marked the seventy-fifth anniversary of
the appearance of the first Guinness advertisement in English
newspapers. It's tempting to let advertising speak for itself in

a chronological order, but if I do that I can't do the brand justice. There is a view from inside the brand: how Guinness people see Guinness through its advertising. There are two views from outside the brand: how advertising agencies see themselves advertising Guinness, and how consumers see Guinness as a result of the other two. For those who want to see Guinness advertising in more linear terms, two books by the same name, *The Book of Guinness Advertising* by Brian Sibley (1985) and Jim Davies (1998), do this brilliantly. Alternatively, there's a great interactive section in the Guinness Storehouse in Dublin. Here, though, I want to tell two stories from different points of view, highlighting very different ways of getting to the end result we call an ad, and showing how these different approaches not only affect that end result but can have massive consequences for the brand.

Guinness is a global brand with different products and advertising in different markets. If we're going to get any idea of the creative tensions that go into Guinness advertising, it's better to look at a small section of one market in detail. In this chapter, I'm mainly looking at Draught Guinness advertising in a UK context.

THOSE FANCY CREATIVES

But first, a positioning statement. There are three stakeholders in the world of advertising: the advertising agency, the client company whose product is being advertised and the consumers who are being advertised to. Advertising agencies are always trying to second-guess your whims and moods and sugar the pill. When they work with heritage brands like

Guinness, they're wary of upsetting your apple cart. Yet quite often that's exactly what they're paid to do. Their task is to shake up your preconceptions and get you to reappraise a product you thought you knew. But why? Well, if you become so absorbed by adorable advertising that you forget to buy the goods, what's the point of advertising in the first place? They'll inevitably want to change it to something that *will* make you want to buy. That's their job.

And your job, as the consumer, is to resist it or go along with it. But your relationship will be with the product or the company that makes it, not the advertising agency that encourages you to have that relationship. All the same, love 'em or hate 'em, ad agencies are the source of some of the most memorable images and ideas you'll ever encounter, including the men with the girder and the Guinness. We can't talk about advertising without discussing the kind of creativity that brings us these unforgettable characters that so influence our lives.

It was a long way from "Guinness is good for you" in 1929 to "Pure genius" in 1987. The first of our two advertising stories starts with a small egg that grew quickly into a mature man.

HOW THEY GOT FROM EGG TO EGO: THE AGENCY STORY OF THE MAN WITH THE GUINNESS

Scotsman Neil Cassie joined Ogilvy & Mather from Hall's in Edinburgh, where he'd had the Tennent's lager account in a market that beat England to the premium draught beer idea. Cassie was the account planner – the man whose job it was to make people work together and take the whole campaign forward. It was 1986, and he already understood the social behaviour and drinking patterns associated with a sector that was just beginning to emerge in England.

O&M's "Genius" advertising had begun. But would it work? Guinness's management had great expectations.

Geniuses

In autumn 1984, the creative review for the £7 million Guinness advertising account lasted three months, cost hundreds of thousands of pounds, was contested by six agencies and was won by a single word. Ogilvy & Mather, the winning agency, had to go through a four-stage process: get on the shortlist, win a pitch place, win a place in the final, win the final.

The winning idea came from two O&M creatives, Mark Wnek and Chris Monge. Locked up in a room in the Savoy Hotel for four days, they ordered room service, hardly slept, and stayed in the same clothes while they racked their brains for the big idea. When it came, it was a word scrawled on a piece of paper in the middle of the night. GENIUS.

Although the genius idea was fantastic, all anybody could talk about was the Guinness egg strategy. Out of six agencies, only O&M had been able to crack the egg brief. But that was the pitch; this was reality.

In summer 1984, disappointed with Allen, Brady & Marsh's "Guinnless" campaign, which focused on people who didn't drink Guinness, Guinness did some research to find out why people *did* drink it. Looking at previous ad campaigns, it discovered that Guinness was a brand with a split personality. Ads that focused on the beer's manly characteristics were hard, like the shell; ads that showed the creamy, warming and nourishing attributes were soft, like the yolk. Trouble was, a

Guinness ad would be one thing or the other, hard or soft. Guinness needed a campaign that embraced both.

Launched in September 1985, Ogilvy & Mather's first attempt to crack the egg for the general public was a two-pronged advertising strategy. One side focused on the type of person likely to drink Guinness (hard shell); the other promoted the values of the product (soft yolk). The ads would alternate to give the big picture, but both would work with the theme of "Genius."

Genius with egg on its face

Four TV ads came out of the egg strategy. "Medallion man" and "Armadillo" were the shell: a bit macho, depicting manly virtues, intended to attract people toward drinking Guinness. "Natural" and "Power" were the yolk: more inward-looking, evoking the brand and the product, its spirit, power and, last but not least, its regenerative properties related to the old idea of "Guinness is good for you." After a couple of months, consumer research showed that the hard-shell ads were not working at all; the soft-yolk "Natural" ad was faring far better than the other three. What did this say about the egg strategy? What did it say about "genius"?

Let Cassie explain in his dulcet Scots tones: "The egg strategy was shite. It made some sort of sense, but it became an albatross. The slavish devotion to the strategy was dominating everything at the expense of the work." As a planner, Cassie was in search of a clue, a sign that would allow his creative team to find the way forward. "My view was that the brand was so rich. If you could seduce consumers with the power of the brand, they would come."

Just as another wave of egg ads was due, Cassie got a hook from Milward Brown, a research-tracking agency. In the

"Natural" ad, people were noticing a flash of a man with a bare torso, standing with a sheaf of barley in a fire. Who was this enigmatic figure? Cassie thought about the Guinness heritage: the toucan and the iron girder, all the iconic advertising that reflected the strength and quality of the brand. Words came: "Guinness is the only draught you can recognize in a glass. It's black and white." Light dawned. The hairs on the back of his neck stood up. "That's what people are seeing. The Guinness heritage!"

Cassie and his researcher, Roy Langley, talked to the black community, where they knew Guinness had a heritage. They started to get a sense of Guinness's power. Men made comments about Guinness sustaining an erection; women noticed how the pint ejaculated at the end of the ad. It all added up to a feeling of sexual potency, mystical power and physical strength.

So there was the mythic figure in black and white supported by a masculine power. But there was more. The other piece of the picture came from drinking Guinness in an Irish bar, where the craic is good and where Guinness loosens you up in a way no other drink can. The more Guinness you drink, the more wisdom – "genius" – you think you're talking.

Cassie was getting more and more excited about this man with heritage, potency and the ability to speak the truths of your soul. But he had to create a brief for a creative team that wouldn't stop talking egg. He saw it as his role to smash the egg and capture the feeling of being engaged with the brand. How could he get the O&M team to feel that? He started to interview them individually about moments when they were absolutely at one with their emotions – that movie, that time, that song, when you lose it and become closest to yourself, when you could cry, when you're in love with the moment.

Smashing the egg
In an O&M meeting room, Neil Cassie collected together materials that reflected what people had told him: music, film posters, whatever. In the middle of the room, he placed a bowl of eggs, one of which was hard boiled. He called the team in and said, "From this moment on, the Guinness brand is no longer about the egg." He started throwing eggs at the wall, smashing them all over the place. Everyone was stunned. Cassie threw the last egg at immaculately dressed account director Miles Young, who thought it was going to explode all over him. It was the hard-boiled one. Miles caught it but stormed out, upset. He said later that it was more like a pop concert than a brief. But the others in the team began to feel the potency and the strength in the details. It was as if they were part of a secret.

Cassie was simply asking his creative team to stop trying to do ads about the consumer and the yolk. "You don't need to advertise this brand in the way others do. Mythical brands don't do advertising. They just are. This is genius."

Was the team inspired? The pressure on it to deliver was growing intolerable. Miles Young was handling the client superlatively. But what did his bunch of 28-year-old creatives know about life?

Ideas were stirring. Chris Monge (he of the "Genius" duo) had been to the theatre and seen *Death of a Salesman* staged inside compartments of Willy Loman's head. It struck a chord with Cassie, who told Monge, "Just do something that enables you to walk right into it, like Willy Loman's head." But this sounded like lunacy. Not just lunacy – heresy. And the pressure was getting worse.

The team was sitting around the office one morning when Monge, who could spot an idea, turned to Mark Wnek (his "Genius" partner), and said, "Tell them!" Wnek explained that he had been watching *The Twilight Zone* the night before, and the Man in Black had walked across the screen talking to him. Cassie jumped up and cried out: "That's it, that's genius! Talking to you directly. He gives you a view on life."

So the Man in Black was born. Wnek and Monge began shaping ideas into parodies of life that were thoughts that go on inside your head, like radio. Guinness went ballistic. What about the egg? O&M was threatened with losing the account. But Langley said it was the best thing they had ever researched.

Guinness demanded that O&M put its best copywriter onto the egg strategy to produce another set of ads for proper research, alongside the Man in Black theme. In the research sessions, the Man in Black idea wiped the other ads away. Guinness came to see for itself how people were reacting to ads like "The university of life" and lines like "Who am I? Pay attention. I may be asking questions." The company still considered the whole approach too highbrow, too upmarket. They insisted O&M did its research among the C to D drinkers who would ultimately make the difference.

Cassie recounts: "We were in a room in Manchester with tattooed lorry drivers. They'd had some beers. Roy Langley ran some trial ads. Half way through, this giant man stood up and started to get really angry and shout, 'I don't know what this is!' Roy said to him in front of everyone, 'Are you angry because you find the man sexually attractive?' All the anger went out of him. He said, 'I'm not saying I'm a poof, but, you know when you're in a pub and you meet someone and you feel you've known them all your life...?"'

An unresearchable phenomenon
Milward Brown analyzed the campaign. It was controversial, because it broke every rule of advertising. It didn't sell the brand at all. It featured a man who spoke no sense whatsoever. There were no drinking scenes. No women. The name "Guinness" was never mentioned. It didn't communicate. Which meant it couldn't shift attitudes. Yet it got branding recognition of 94 percent. It was the Man in Black with white hair. People could tell you about the man with the dolphin, but not what it meant. Yet the campaign *had* shifted attitude – more so than any campaign Milward Brown had ever monitored. "Congratulations, gentlemen; you have broken the mould. But we have no idea why it works. Our research model does not fit your campaign. You have a phenomenon on your hands."

Guinness had to accept. It actually became a zealot in the end. For O&M, it was all down to great client management: creating work that broke the mould, but making sure the client felt they owned it and it fitted the brief.

Guinness wanted the ads made immediately. By this time O&M had given the Man in Black a name: John Priest. They looked at spaced-out English actors, but they couldn't get the right person. People didn't want the role. The Guinness Distillers affair was all over the front pages. O&M were stuck.

You'd think lots of people would rush to claim responsibility for finding the man who made the biggest difference to Guinness since John Gilroy. Not so. Cassie said it was the media planner on the account, Neil Quick, who went to see the film *Blade Runner*, came back and said, "There's this guy called Rutger Hauer, and he is John Priest."

But Rutger Hauer was not the way the team had envisaged John Priest. They couldn't get beyond the idea of an English intellectual. They were looking for brainy guys, not brawny guys. But when they went to see Rutger Hauer with some scripts, he said in his inimitable way, "I want to do this." "So we had this guy who was like a psychopath with a sense of humour. When the first ad appeared in June 1987, they sold out of Guinness on the first day," recalls Cassie.

Was the idea bigger than Rutger Hauer? O&M would say yes, because it researched so well before he had even been cast. Yet who else could have combined brawn with brain? Ah, he was only an actor. And Guinness was only a beer.

And Foster's was only a beer too. Paul Hogan was already in place for that brand, but the Man in Black personified values in a way that only Guinness could: with depth and humour and substance, and with a touch of the enigmatic. Guinness had permission to be a little bit different. Rutger Hauer was completely believable. In the role, he made it cool and attractive for mid- to late-20s guys to drink Guinness. For the agency, he was the Man in Black. For the public and posterity, he would always be The Man with the Guinness.

Between 1987 and 1994, the Ogilvy & Mather ads helped boost Guinness's share of the beer market to its highest level for 20 years. One in 20 pints served was Guinness. Guinness had effortlessly set a style of its own and spawned enigmatic copycats. But what do you do once everybody has caught up? By 1994, everyone had. It was time for Guinness to move on and face the next bout between creativity and strategy.

EXPRESSING THAT INNER CONFIDENCE: HOW GUINNESS PEOPLE GOT TO "BELIEVE"

For the purposes of comparison, move forward to the year 2000. Guinness has become part of Diageo. Sales are in decline. The new Guinness global brand team begins a radical rethink of the whole Guinness message and approach to communicating it.

After Jon Potter, Guinness's global brand director, David Cunningham was the second person to join the team. His brief? To do the advertising, brand positioning and strategy work. No small task. As he says: "Guinness had lots of different markets with lots of different advertising, working with different advertising agencies, communicating lots of different things."

Abbott Mead Vickers BBDO had taken over the Guinness account in 1998 after Ogilvy & Mather had run a controversial campaign, "Not everything in black and white makes sense," as their big idea following on from The Man with the Guinness. Even before the campaign began, there were huge rumours that Guinness was about to feature the first gay kiss in a British TV ad. The tabloid press got hold of it: "My goodness, my gayness" ran one headline. The Guinness management took fright. The ad was pulled and another was run in its place. The relationship with Ogilvy & Mather never recovered. So far, AMV BBDO had produced three ads in their first campaign, "Good things come to those who wait." Two of the three, "Surfer" and "Swimblack," were critically acclaimed. A fourth, "Dream club," was due out in spring 2001. But huge changes were afoot in the world of Guinness advertising.

Surfer

"Surfer" was voted best-ever ad in a competition run by the UK's Channel 4 and *The Times* in London. Director Jonathan Glazer explains: "The idea was to make something quite extraordinary happen on a TV screen. We wanted something cinematic and hypnotic, but with a certain poetry to it."[3] "Surfer" took three months to produce, including 12 days shooting the surfers in Hawaii. Sixty people were involved, including a location crew of 25 and two Lipizaner horses. The ad was in post-production for more than two months, where the latest computer technology was used to weave the horses seamlessly into the crashing surf, with the help of the hypnotic music of Leftfield. The final edit was signed off just 30 minutes before the ad went out for the first time.

ONE GLOBAL BRAND, ONE GLOBAL VISION

Working with new branding rules from parent company Diageo, Guinness had the twin tasks of reducing its roster of global advertising agencies down to one, and finding a unified global vision to communicate in every market.

Dweeb

Diageo's global brand strategy team is nicknamed Dweeb: the Diageo way of brand building. It devises ways of building brands effectively on a global scale. It brings together the right people from the right areas of the business to work together collaboratively in stages. The whole idea is to get everyone disciplined into thinking of the brand in terms of marketing. Dweeb creates a line of logic that runs from what Diageo calls the key brand benefit to a communications idea and on to the advertising execution.

Guinness had several agencies at the time: Saatchi's for Africa, AMV BBDO for the UK, HHCL in Ireland, two in America, O&M in Asia, a couple of others in France and Germany. How on earth to get these down to one? It couldn't run a creative review, as it had on many previous occasions, because it hadn't done the brand positioning work yet. It didn't have a strategy, or anything to measure the agencies against. So it simply dropped the smaller agencies in the US and Europe, knowing that they would never be able to supply the global network. That left AMV BBDO and Saatchi's. But with one agency advertising Guinness Draught and the other advertising Guinness Foreign Extra Stout, how could you choose between them?

David Cunningham set up a team including all the major market directors to look at the two remaining agencies.

Everyone with a stake in the decision had a seat at the table. There was some bitterness among the agencies, and a lot of internal controversy and external interest. How had Guinness got down to these two agencies? But everyone pulled together because they felt they had to for the benefit of the new Diageo company. The big question remained: could Guinness get to one agency?

TWO GLOBAL AGENCIES, ONE GLOBAL VISION

Just before Christmas 2000, Guinness announced that it could not go for a single agency. The question was: creativity or global reach? People were convinced of Saatchi's creativity and satisfied with its global reach, but it had only handled Guinness Foreign Extra Stout. AMV BBDO had affiliations all around the world and had experienced some success with the prestigious Guinness Draught, but it had no network in Africa to handle Foreign Extra Stout.

So the decision boiled down to giving the lot to Saatchi's or keeping two agencies. The result surprised no one. Guinness was happy; it had got down to two agencies. The marketing press saw it mainly as a cop-out. Was Guinness putting pragmatism and safety ahead of the brave choice of one creative direction? How typical that a large company should do this – but was it a good thing for Guinness? One or two journalists who understood the two different Guinness worlds of Draught and Foreign Extra Stout saw the decision as the inevitable compromise it was. This was life under Diageo. How was Guinness going to make its situation work?

At the time, the company had at least eight different key brand benefits from around the Guinness world. The task was to find a single unifying global positioning statement: the strongest, most pertinent thing to say about the brand. Perhaps the best example was in Africa, where new advertising was growing the market phenomenally using the slogan "Guinness brings out the power in you." But it applied only to Foreign Extra Stout.

LET THE CONSUMERS CHOOSE

The internal politics were evident from the beginning. Market directors hadn't been involved in the agency selection. Some were losing their agencies. They'd sweated to develop and control their own key brand benefits. Said David Cunningham: "The important thing was to enlist them and get them to be objective. So we didn't set a single key brand benefit, communication idea or advertising idea as our goal, even though we'd been asked to do that. We said we'd use consumers and research to tell us what is and isn't possible."

The material to put into research went through a series of big global workshops, looking at different brand positionings and consumer research. The Diageo way of brand building was taking firm hold. One theme came through loud and clear: strength. Africa was already interpreting this idea in an overtly physical way, drawing on a long heritage and the current advertising featuring Michael Power. The UK approach had more to do with body and soul; the "Swimblack" and "Surfer" ads showed people doing extraordinary things, so that the vision emerged here as "inner strength."

AFRICA ALREADY HAD SELF-BELIEF

After they'd successfully put inner strength out to research in nine markets, Guinness then asked both agencies to find one idea that would express inner strength in everything from global advertising to internal communications. They would be working together for the first time. Inevitably, the agencies saw this as a creative pitch in which they were competing against each other. They came back with different ideas, but also some duplication.

There was no getting away from the fact that there were two communication ideas expressing inner strength. Africa was advertising Guinness Foreign Extra Stout under the slogan "Guinness brings out the power in you" and using Michael Power to represent a real-life hero who embodies all the good things about Guinness. But, representing the physical world of Africa, would he be relevant in the mental world of Asia? The issue was about getting the nuance right. Africa did not see any need to change, so it was down to Asia to find a solution for its FES advertising. Cunningham recalls, " Africa said, let them develop it. If it's better than Michael Power, we'll move to it." But Asia couldn't find its own idea. Guinness decided to take the idea of Michael Power and adapt it for Asia, and developed an Asian character called Adam King in the same spirit.

The second communication idea was the one used for Guinness Draught: dramatizing moments of self-belief and the positive impact they have on oneself and others. You establish the hero, set a challenge, show doubt, resolution, celebration. When someone incorporated the Guinness harp as the letter "v" in the word "Believe", they knew they had something. With the FES markets of Africa and Asia sorted, the rest of the Guinness (Draught) world was left to take up "Believe" as its global communication idea. It was used overtly in advertising in the UK, Ireland, the US and Australia, and was woven into existing African FES advertising and the new Asian advertising based on the African model.

GOT A BRIEF, GET AN AD

From the beginning, inner strength gave Guinness trouble; it was hard to express it in an ad. Through their actions, someone shows they have immense belief in themselves. It's not confidence; that can be showy or arrogant. It's self-belief. Only you know if you have it or not. It's the key thing for success in life – whatever that means. Guinness also needed to show how someone's inner strength can have a positive impact on other people. It couldn't just be an individual thing.

The advertising brief about "dramatising moments of self-belief" went out to AMV network agencies in the four critical Guinness Draught markets: the UK, Ireland, the US and Australia. All were given three weeks to come back with scripts. Even though the agencies were told to filter out their weaker ideas, this still produced 36 scripts. Twenty of them were presented in a single day. It was creative overload for Cunningham and his team.

What got the team through? According to Cunningham, it was the last of the four AMV ads based on "Good things come to those who wait." "'Dream club' was so hated in the UK that it gave us a great burst of incentive at the time. It aided the politics immensely."

Dream club

"Dream club" is one of the least understood Guinness ads of recent times, and consequently one of the most talked about. An anonymous man sits in an anonymous pub somewhere in an anonymous Eastern European country. He dreams as he waits for his drink, or he drinks while he waits for his dream. Tonight it's the big one; the question we all want the answer to. What is the meaning of life? Shot in Budapest in December 2000, the ad wasn't finished until the day of the first transmission in March 2001; writer Walter Campbell made tweaks to the dialogue and music right up to the last minute. Director Jonathan Glazer blamed the squirrels for making the ad take so long in production.

AT THE END OF THE DAY, SOME ADS

"Believe" and a five-part script construction (establish the hero, set a challenge, show some doubt, provide the resolution, launch the celebration) became the basis of the three ads that followed: "Free-in," "Lava" and "Tom Crean."

In research, where people are shown animatics or preliminary versions of an ad, "Free-in" scored higher than the award-winning "Surfer" or "Swimblack." As the first ad, it was the cue for celebration all around. It seemed to confirm that "Believe" – the single global communication idea developed by AMV and Saatchi's – was working, at least across all Guinness Draught markets.

Free-in
The first Guinness ad to be screened in all four major Draught markets, "Free-in" was also the first execution of the global campaign "Believe," based on the brand vision of inner strength. Created by Irish International, part of the AMV BBDO group, it was directed by Vaughan Arnell, critically acclaimed for his Carlsberg, Stella and Levi's ads and videos for Robbie Williams and George Michael. In hurling, a free-in is a free kick or penalty kick. In the ad, it's right at the end of the game. In the free-in taker's mind, it's win or bust, with the prospect of a Guinness celebration.

After a mixed reception, two other "Believe" ads were made, but not screened in all markets. The idea of dramatizing inner moments of self-belief was felt to be too difficult to execute.

The second ad, "Lava", scored even higher than "Free-in" in research. In its original animatic form, it had humour, colour and a powerful soundtrack, "Fire" by the Crazy World of Arthur Brown. Irish International wanted to make the final ad as close to the animatic as possible, but AMV London had

"Lava"

the final say, and the end product turned out to be very different. At one stage, Guinness and AMV were sidetracked by the possibility of getting Ridley Scott to direct it, hard on the heels of *Gladiator*, but it never happened. Cunningham: "So in the end we got a very different film and it had lost an element of its warmth, through having no colour or soundtrack. There was a big event going on in the ad. But we lost the group thing. It was dark and dingy. We'd wanted a colour ad. We got a sepia ad." "Lava" was shown only in Great

Britain and Ireland. The third ad in the series, "Tom Crean," was shown only in Ireland.

ONE GLOBAL VISION, BUT TOTAL MARKET FLEXIBILITY

Following his exertions, David Cunningham took a year away from the Guinness global brand team. When he returned in 2002, he discovered the pendulum had swung back again in the approach to advertising. "We still have one global key brand benefit, but we are allowing flexibility. Having one global vision is fine, but expression can differ. It's such a big discussion: that markets should have flexibility to find their own way. Having said that, none have come through with anything that works. With inner strength, it remains a huge creative challenge to show something that's 'inner.'"

Today, he wonders whether Guinness has again created several local key brand benefits. "Letting agencies work on local experiences and turn them to their advantage, we could go back to where we were. On the other hand, we might get the best of both worlds with inner strength. We now have a smaller team of people to take more risks."

How Diageo sees this is another matter. Does it have the appetite for risky advertising?

CREATIVITY OR STRATEGY?

The two examples of "The Man with the Guinness" and "Believe" show how complicated Guinness finds its own brand. They also show how difficult it can be for an advertising agency to interpret a Guinness brief.

Neil Quick began as O&M media planner on the Guinness account before becoming account director. "The egg strategy was intellectually rigorous, but ultimately not likely to lead to coherent advertising. For good creative work you have to believe that a concept is executable. And the creative work that came out of the egg wasn't that good. It was the Man with the Guinness execution that unified the brand, rather than the strategy."

Brian Pate was advertising manager for Guinness during the development of the egg strategy and The Man with the Guinness: "Some ads tell you what to think; the two "Believe" ads do. I believe two million percent that Guinness advertising needs to be enigmatic, surreal, challenging, multi-layered, but with an easy access point, with its hard and soft strands working together and not telling you what to think."

Neil Cassie smashed the Guinness egg strategy to get to the truth of the brand: "This is a leading brand – one that constantly innovates in the way it comes to you. "Dream club" was closest to the truth of the brand and the relationship people have with it. "Surfer" was brilliant and deserved its awards, but didn't capture it emotionally for me. "Believe" is shite. It says it, but doesn't make you feel it."

John Wheelhouse was Guinness's advertising manager during The Man with the Guinness series: "So much of modern drinks advertising is not rooted in the truth of the brand. If you take an ad, then cut it ten seconds before the end, it might be a car ad, or for a bank. But Guinness has to be rooted in truth, meet people's needs and be relevant to people at a certain time."

Jon Eggleton was Guinness's advertising manager during the controversial "Not everything in black and white makes sense" campaign in 1996/97: "The Man with the Guinness was the most successful ad campaign Guinness ever ran. It totally changed perceptions of Guinness. But the classic advertising rule is to take a unique product attribute and dramatize it. 'Believe' concerns me. What does it say about Guinness as a product?"

David Cunningham was in charge of the "Believe" advertising: "Have we lost some element of creative brilliance? That is the most pertinent question. The Diageo striving for this line of logic can squeeze out creative brilliance. Our challenge was to keep stuff with a spark of brilliance and get everyone to buy in, which can reduce risk taking. I wish we had taken more risk. If good ideas didn't get great support from consumers, we weren't brave enough to put them through."

In today's competitive marketplace, it's doubtful whether Guinness's current advertising agency in draught markets, AMV BBDO, sees itself as capable of challenging Guinness in the way that Ogilvy & Mather did in 1986. But the opportunity is still there.

WHERE DOES GUINNESS STAND TODAY?

In 2001, Guinness global brand director Jon Potter described "Believe" as Guinness's "first global advertising campaign since the 1930s." Since then, he has learned that "Believe" is far more than the advertising that comes out of it. "We thought 'Believe' was the destination and the solution, but it is actually a journey. It has values that are global at the heart of it, but it needs local execution. We thought we had the answer, but we had found the start. At least we know where we're starting from. What the creativity looks like is the challenge. How do we reinvent it? I feel very comfortable about where we are, even though we're back with the markets running their own ads. But the confidence belief thing is now so embedded. It's how you create it."

Potter believes that by going down a global branding route, Guinness has unlocked a valuable truth: that advertising has a bigger role to play than just communicating brand positioning. Yes, it drives the way people engage with the brand. But it can also drive the way Guinness innovates on quality, and how it responds to social and cultural occasions from the Rugby World Cup to St Patrick's Day. Thanks to all the work it has done on the global truth of Guinness, it now has a much deeper understanding of how the different elements of the mix work. That said, Guinness's advertising remains an experiment of 75 years' duration.

With so many years under its belt, Guinness advertising is as much a product of the brand as Draught Guinness itself. This works both for and against the company. On the one hand, people know and love the advertising and expect more of this witty entertainment; woe betide Guinness if it deprives them. On the other hand, people's affection for the ads doesn't always stretch to handing over the money in their pockets. After all, it isn't obligatory, and there are lots of other calls on their resources, as well as persuasive voices making them.

For one reason or another the product will change, and in the clamour of voices from other products doing exactly the same, there is only one way to be heard: shout. Not shout louder, but shout differently. That's the Guinness way.

Guinness advertising through the years has never been loud and brash, but always clever and careful, where "careful" means relevant, painstaking and responsible.

WHAT TO THINK?

Power, goodness and a third element, communion, are the values that underpin Guinness's vision of itself as the global brand of inner strength. All Guinness advertising has to reflect these values if it is to reflect inner strength. But with "Believe," Guinness clearly had trouble making its advertising potent and effective.

It's always easy to blame execution. Only time will tell whether inner strength is the factor that unites the world of Guinness.

Source: Message left on the "Home" wall of postcards by a visitor to the Guinness Storehouse in Dublin, 28 November 2003

Though the global brand team is confident that it represents the first step in the brand's next journey, I believe the jury is still out.

To me, power, goodness and communion are enough in themselves to project Guinness anywhere in the world. It will always have power – the blackness, bitterness and strength that Guinness drinkers can associate with feeling confident, experienced and in control. It will always have goodness – as long as it continues to be based on its four natural ingredients. It will always have communion – even though Guinness itself sometimes struggles to understand what this means. Yet it's the communion element that gives Guinness the flexibility to adapt with the time and the audience. I believe the secret of great Guinness advertising lies in the way it attunes communion to the times in which we live.

So, to these eyes, ears and senses, inner strength is an idea too far, an unnecessary step beyond power, goodness and

Communion

Sharing or holding in common; participation; community; fellowship; common action. All are standard dictionary definitions of communion. Shared feelings are meaningful feelings. In 1987, Rutger Hauer showed us how a strong man can have communion with himself. In 1994, Irish actor Joe McKinney showed us how a young man can have communion with his beer as he danced around his surging pint to the memorable music of Perez Prado in the "Anticipation" ad. Today, Guinness Adorers have communion with the brand. And the Guinness brand seeks communion with all its consumers.

It's not so difficult to see how communion works, or where it comes from. Guinness produces and markets a product that tastes distinctive, is perceived to improve well-being and encourages a universal kind of social enjoyment. With Guinness, there's even a spiritual dimension. The Guinness family split early on into three branches: bankers, brewers and missionaries. Power, goodness and communion. Amen.

communion. It doesn't surprise me that AMV's creative agencies have had difficulties executing it. We've seen how Guinness arrived at inner strength. Why couldn't they have left it at strength? That would have allowed a wider range of executions to take place: strength of character, mind, will, spirit. Or would that have left Guinness open to criticism that it was simply reverting to a 1930s idea that advertising standards would no longer tolerate? How do you show that it's people with strength who drink Guinness, as opposed to drinking Guinness to get strength?

This is a tough call for Guinness, beset as it is by pressures to produce advertising that encourages responsible drinking. For a while, we were left dangling in mid-air, wondering how Guinness was going to find the next way of expressing something as invisible as inner strength. Hundreds of scripts poured in from the worldwide AMV network, but nothing quite got there. Until now. After belief comes confidence.

OUT OF DARKNESS COMES LIGHT

At last, is Guinness's advertising beginning to display the self-belief it has been promoting? "Out of darkness comes light" is the end-line of the new campaign launched in the UK in February 2004. The key brand benefit of inner strength takes a step back. Guinness is moving away from an idea that it found difficult to express without suggesting that Guinness fuels inner belief. New marketing codes, both internal and external, demand that Guinness merely symbolizes, not fuels. Next time I go down the pub I must remember to order my symbolic pint of Guinness. I wouldn't mind; it's just that they'll want real money for it. Joking aside, the difficulties of executing ads about inner strength in the climate of moral probity and responsible drinking in the US, Ireland and increasingly the UK, have finally produced a different approach.

There are two big differences between the "Out of darkness comes light" and "Believe" ads. The first and most important is that AMV has put a crucial truth about the product at the heart of the story: the dark beer surges and settles to produce a contrasting light head. Second, drinking Guinness is a relaxing experience. Where "Believe" had its heroes grappling with mental strength, the first "Out of darkness" ad, "Moth," has its hero instinctively following a cloud of moths that lead him and his friends out of the forest and, happily, toward the shining lights of a jazz bar. With the moths representing the surge and mystery of the dark beer and the lightness representing the drinking experience, a Guinness ad is again focusing on what it really means to be a Guinness drinker. But is the idea powerful enough? Does "Out of the darkness comes light" have legs? We shall see.

It's just as well, then, that it turns out that inner strength is an idea that works much better in Africa, where advertising

"Moth"

is less sophisticated and less regulated. In the UK and Ireland, it is too far removed from the reasons why people drink beer. In Australia, they didn't even see the problem. No worries, just celebrate when you win (and Australians usually win). When people go to the pub they want to relax. They don't want to get into all that heavy introspective stuff about decisive moments. Yes, Guinness has a heritage of strength, but drinking Guinness is about relaxing and enjoying yourself. Strength reveals itself better through the confidence to be yourself in ordinary situations rather than in dramatic decisive moments in extraordinary ones.

Guinness is known for clever, humorous ads, but from time to time it needs to focus on a simple product truth. Now, of course, a Guinness ad is expected to do that cleverly, too. Once again, it's time for a product truth. As the surge settles, out of darkness comes light. There's hope here. AMV is returning to the simple ideas that won it the Guinness account in 1998. It inherited the account from Ogilvy & Mather, whose controversial "Not everything in black and white makes sense" campaign caused Guinness too many problems. Critics said it contained no product truths. It *did* contain a product truth: it's black and white, but not as black and white as you think. That rings a bell, doesn't it? It just didn't show people drinking the product as much as it might have done.

BACKWARD TO GO FORWARD?

Is there a way for Guinness to go backward to go forward? Maybe. But just as we can't go back to a world before mobile phones, we can't revert to a life without global branding initiatives, vision statements and key brand benefits. All of them are here to stay. But we do have to ask ourselves what we've lost. For Guinness, or rather its agencies, the answer may well be creative freedom.

Today, notwithstanding 75 years of brilliant advertising heritage, it's harder than ever for Guinness's creative agencies to produce something inspiring when so much (too much) of the brand has been dissected, forensically examined and minutely labelled. So little is left to be discovered, including, alas, some of the mystery that makes the brand what it is. In the mystery lies the myth: the material for the parables. Guinness spends a lot of effort destroying myths. Without mystery and myth there can be no genius.

Neil Quick: "What's dogged people throughout the years is that Guinness is Guinness is Guinness. When they attempt to overextend the brand it pulls things away." From what matters; from the truth of the myth.

Watch this space
Not many advertising agencies today get three chances to get something right. When they had their creative freedom, AMV BBDO started well with "Good things come to those who wait." When they had to fight for the right to execute "Believe," things didn't work out so well. For their third attempt, will AMV get the creative space to do advertising justice to one of the world's greatest brands? If we are to have the first golden age of Guinness advertising since 1994, AMV will have to be at its very best.

Notes
1   "AMV Guinness win seals position as dominant agency," Stefano Hatfield, *Campaign*, 16 January 1998.
2   *The Book of Guinness Advertising*, Jim Davies, Guinness Publishing, 1998, p9.
3   "A touch of the extraordinary," Guinness *Globe* magazine, June 2000.

INWARD
IRISHNESS

They're digging up the roads in Dublin. The tramlines are going down. The logjam traffic that characterizes this city in flux has brought my taxi to a standstill. We talk Guinness.

"And that reminds me of something that somebody said to Brendan Behan," says the taxi driver. "'Hasn't Guinness been good to the people of Dublin?' And Brendan Behan took a slow drink and wiped his mouth and looked the man in the eye and said, 'And haven't the people of Dublin been good to Guinness?'"

Before you get anywhere in Dublin you're already getting the Irishness that can never be explained, only explored; never portrayed, only performed. And it just gets better.

Barman: "Who ordered the pint and a half of Guinness?"

Me: "I did – and how much is that?"

Barman: "How should I know? Just give me some money and I'll give you some change."

And the price of a pint of Guinness in Dublin is 4 euros, and the price of a half is 3 euros. Not everything in black and white makes sense. Especially when it's not as black and white as that.

GUINNESS IS A FACT OF LIFE

In Ireland, Guinness enters any conversation as a fact of life. To draw a comparison, make a point, get the next one in. From a young age, Irish people learn about the beer, the birds and the bees. In that order. The beer comes first and the beer is Guinness. Fact. Of life. In Ireland.

But sometimes, at the height of passion or in the depths of despair, you can forget the facts of life. That's exactly what

Guinness
made me
pregnant.
Cheers
Ireland!

Source: Message left on the "Home" wall of postcards by a visitor
to the Guinness Storehouse in Dublin, 28 November 2003

happened to Guinness in Ireland during the 1990s. It forgot
who loved it and went after who didn't. Its heart was in the
wrong place. The people it chased so hard didn't want to know,
and the people it left behind were exactly that, left behind.

Today, if you go the Guinness Storehouse in Dublin –
only 5 percent of visitors are Irish – you'll see a proud
representation of Guinness as the Irish brand. If you are at all
of a philosophical bent, you might say that the Storehouse
promotes Irishness as much as it does Guinness. And you'd
have little or no idea that, until a very recent rekindling of
affection, Guinness and the people of Ireland had fallen out of
love with each other. Ah well, the Storehouse is a tourist

The Guinness Storehouse

attraction; gotta present the right face and all. Is that right? Once more, a little bit of history can focus our perspective.

CELTIC TIGER, TOOTHLESS BEER

To cut a long story short, since the mid-1980s the Irish economy has moved from second-world to first-world ranking. As Dublin continues to transform itself into an international city and twenty-first century trams hurtle along its wide Georgian avenues, Ireland grows in stature. Here we have the rise of the Celtic tiger and with it the pull of the old Ireland and the push of the new.

And where was Guinness in all this thrusting change? Firmly in the vanguard, trying to capture all that was new, including lager-drinking younger consumers raised on higher expectations and rapid change. Yet for twenty solid years, sales of Draught Guinness slipped and nobody bothered to get down to the truth, because every other pint of stout sold in Ireland was Guinness and everyone knew it was tattooed on the national psyche anyway.

Guinness was selling more volume, but only on the back of the overall explosion in beer sales led by lager. Besides, since the late 1980s the company had distributed Budweiser and brewed Carlsberg in Ireland, adding to overall profits, but masking the loss in Draught Guinness. And if population statistics were to be believed – and they were – a demographic explosion of young people seemed to call for a different approach to marketing for an established brand like Guinness.

The big pint

It fell to London-based advertising agency, Howell Henry Chaldecott Lury & Partners to take over the long tradition of its Irish predecessor, Arks, in Ireland. Its brief was to attract younger customers so that Guinness would grow in the long term. HHCL's first major campaign was "The big pint," a strategy based on size, substance, taste, texture and worth, expressed in immediate, relevant and surprising ways, but also with humour. Marketing director Tim Kelly knew that Guinness in Ireland mustn't be seen as an older person's drink, yet mustn't look so young that it frightened off older drinkers. It was out with the old product language of "velvety, creamy, smooth, dark" which meant nothing to 18-year-olds and sounded dated, and in with words like "taste-tackler," describing the product with a touch of humour.

This attempt to express the past with relevance fell flat on its face. New drinkers didn't like it; Guinness Adorers hated it. Kelly had said there was more to Guinness than other pints: more taste, more texture, more reward. His mistake was to imply that "You can't have your pint and drink it," which of course every Irish Guinness drinker can.

What had worked in the advertising of the 1970s would not work for the sharp 1990s. No more waiting for the curragh to arrive at the shore with the island's long-awaited keg. But plenty more ways how to dance with a pint of it and live life to the power of Guinness.

BETWEEN A ROCK AND A HARD PLACE

Thankfully, Guinness today is caught between tradition and the contemporary. This is no half-way house or no-man's-land. For Guinness in Ireland, it is the only place to be. To paraphrase former marketing director Steve Langan, Guinness has learned how to value tradition but step beyond it. And how has it managed that?

In current brand controller Mark Ody, has Guinness discovered a basic truth that is all the harder to swallow because it comes from an Englishman? Namely, that it is high time the Guinness brand in Ireland learned to fall in love with itself all over again? And why shouldn't it take an Englishman to tell Irishmen how to love their most famous brand? The English have been inundated by Irishness this past decade and longer, as sold to them by brands such as Caffrey's, the Ireland football team, Boyzone, Michael Flatley and, yes, the Irish pub phenomenon. Whereas in Ireland itself, the Guinness brand has associated itself with everything *except* what is Irish about it, all in the name of recruiting irreverent young Ireland. With 75 percent of the marketing spend going on attracting difficult young drinkers, is it any wonder that older Adorers became disenfranchised? But as English marketing directors before Ody have discovered, it's fine to know what Ireland needs, but very difficult to provide what Ireland wants. And *vice versa*.

When Tim Kelly started in Ireland in the mid-1990s, someone asked him, "Are you going to be a recruitment or a reassurance marketing director?" What they meant was, "Are you going to attract new customers or hold on to existing ones?" Kelly was quick to point out that he didn't see it as an either/or decision. With HHCL on board, it was under Kelly that Guinness began putting greater effort into targeting both: splitting the marketing effort across different age groups and sponsoring hurling on the one hand and opera on the other. "We walk a tightrope every day between trying to attract someone in a language, a tone and with a message that's relevant to them without upsetting someone else."[1]

Of course, in our age of market segmentation where a brand has different ads for different audiences, we might ask: why couldn't Guinness get *both* markets right? Surely it should have been able to appeal to younger drinkers as well as retaining older ones? For a brand that was approaching its 250th anniversary, that shouldn't have been rocket science. But it all comes down to the right creative executions at the right time, backed up by genuine market innovation by Guinness toward customers, in bars, at home, wherever they drink. And it was difficult to get it right.

Ireland was growing as it had never done before. It was virgin territory for everyone. Guinness might have been slowly leaking sales, but it was still dominant in the marketplace. And things had always been done differently in Ireland. Advertising wasn't just about boosting keg sales. That was important, but so was keeping Guinness in the minds and hearts of local communities the length and breadth of the country, as the company had always done. Call it a brilliant marketing strategy if you must, but Guinness has a history of benevolence in Ireland that has its roots in the family who founded the company in the middle of the eighteenth century.

UNCLE ARTHUR'S COMMUNITY SPIRIT

In the early days, the sponsorship strategy – although Guinness would never have called it that – was driven by the need to connect with and develop communities. Within a century, Guinness was at the centre of many community activities in Irish towns and villages, encouraging economic growth, supporting social initiatives, maintaining the balance in times of political upheaval. The benevolence and patronage of the first Arthur Guinness and his sons and grandsons shone through. Over time, this translated into full-scale sponsorships such as the Guinness Cork Jazz Festival, which is massive, international and part of Guinness past and present.

But Guinness is a modern business that has to ask itself tough questions, such as "Do our sponsorships drive consumer equity? Do they sell more beer?" How hard and unfeeling, you may say. But all corporate benevolence has to operate on the back-scratching principle. When it puts money into a community event, Guinness needs to know if it will gain any commercial value through the number of kegs sold or a better relationship with the local vintners' association. That's how it works. To think otherwise is naïve. It's always been that way.

NICE FACE, SHAME ABOUT THE BEER

When Guinness pulled out of the Rose of Tralee festival in 2002, it didn't take the decision lightly. It had supported this beauty contest for decades. So was it that beauty contests were seen as wrong, or as a thing of the past? The truth was, Guinness never sold enough Guinness at them. Better to put the money into other more modern festivals that do just as well for the community *and* sell some Guinness.

The WitNNESS festival in 2003 probably marked the end of Guinness's ten-year drive to recruit younger drinkers. Guinness has spent 15 million euros on several of the annual WitNNESS festivals, every one of them inspirational, every one recording extremely high prompted and unprompted association with Guinness. Yet according to Mark Ody, "I don't think we've recruited more than 500 drinkers from them." So WitNNESS was another example of failing to capture the younger market. It clearly wasn't for lack of trying.

But the Guinness Ploughing Championship and Guinness Galway Oyster Festival go on. Not forgetting the opera. In 1951, Guinness sponsored the Wexford Opera. The very next year, local vintners wanted their own opera for the masses. So today you have the swinging and singing pub competition. The singing pubs feature traditional Irish music; the swinging pubs have modern music, Bryan Adams-style. So, Guinness is in with the community, in with the vintners, flowing from the taps. It's the nurturing of the common man. Throughout Ireland, all year long.

OCCASIONALITY OCCURS REGULARLY

If the drinking occasion is right, then the event is right. So Guinness is pulling out of WitNNESS. The pop festival experience is all about release (get away, get drunk, get laid, get high one way or another), and Guinness doesn't work in that frame of mind. It's about sitting down with your mates and having a laugh. Guinness's experience of sponsorship opportunities and events has probably taught it more about what it means to people in Ireland than expensive TV advertising ever will.

Guinness marketing people now know that they have to do two things: bring more people into Guinness territory, and take Guinness to where people are. This is new thinking in Ireland. Back in the 1970s, Guinness people used to believe in

Cold truths

In its attempt to recruit new drinkers in the 1990s, Guinness introduced Guinness Draught Extra Cold. Guinness told Irish pub landlords that putting Extra Cold in alongside Draught would raise sales of Guinness overall. But then it found that although Extra Cold worked well in the UK and Northern Ireland, it didn't in Dublin. Extra Cold started out in Ireland in 1994 as Guinness Cold Flow, and suffered from perceptions that the cold was to mask the bitterness. Publicans and journalists hated it. Diageo didn't put a lot behind it. Targeting irreverent young Ireland failed.

Guinness had also believed Extra Cold was an alternative drink for Adorers who didn't want to get out of Guinness, but wanted something cold. That idea crashed too. Extra Cold didn't recruit new drinkers or promote switching among older drinkers. Guinness soon learned that the fate of Extra Cold depended on how ingrained the brand was in people's psyche. In Northern Ireland, where Guinness has a slender 13 percent share of the beer market, Extra Cold works well. In Ireland, where virtually every other pint poured is a Guinness, there is more resistance. Live and learn. Guinness does. It has now pulled Extra Cold from Dublin pubs.

Whale
oil
beef
hooked

Source: Message left on the "Home" wall of postcards by a visitor to the Guinness Storehouse in Dublin, 28 November 2003

the Guinness "Holy Trinity": that people could be moved along the line of its beers from Harp lager to Smithwick's ale to Guinness itself. Today, though, when you go into a bar, there are 15 beers on tap. Other great brands satisfy all the needs that Guinness does.

KEEP ON RE-RECRUITING

So the penny has finally dropped at Guinness. It's not about recruiting, but re-recruiting – a sort of "black to the future." In Ireland, thanks to its heritage and status as one of the facts of life, Guinness is something that most people are open to, so all the company has to do is take it to them. Instead of inventing new ways of getting people to drink Guinness (Draught Guinness In Bottles, FastPour, Extra Cold), it's creating new occasions for them to drink it. In that clumsy way with words marketers sometimes have, they call it "occasionality." Guinness is no longer obsessed with making sure you get the message, as long as you enjoy the experience. The big question for Guinness in Ireland is no longer "How can we get these young people to drink our beer?" but "Where can we go to meet some of these people?"

That isn't to say that Guinness in Ireland is turning its back on TV advertising. Now that it's learned to love itself and its Adorers once more, it can't wait to produce the next phase of advertising to celebrate this reconnection. But again, TV advertising during these high-flying economic years has been something that Guinness has had to learn the hard way.

It's sad to see the recent demise of Arks, the old Dublin advertising agency that held the Guinness account until 1995, first in association with Benson's and then by itself. In many ways, the history of Guinness advertising in Ireland is the history of Arks. In 2001, *Marketing* magazine held a survey to find the Irish ad of the century, Arks had four nominations in the top 16, and won the poll with its 1977 "Island" ad for Guinness. It featured three men rowing a keg of stout to expectant islanders. In it, time seemed to stand still.

The award was a swansong for Arks, which seemed to understand better than anyone else that it was always the Irishness of Guinness that enriched the brand, for young people and for their fathers and for their fathers before them. For Guinness, it was a sign once and for all that it must always be in tune with Irish tradition.

AN IRISH "LEAP"YEAR

The year 2001 marked a turning point for Guinness. It won Advertiser of the Year at the Clio Awards in Miami for its advertising in Ireland, the UK, South Africa, the US, Malaysia and Singapore. Clio, the world's largest and most famous international advertising competition, had given this top award only three times in 42 years: to Volvo, Adidas and Volkswagen.

In London, the award was played down. Guinness had always won advertising awards. What was more important was the effectiveness of the advertising. Besides, here was international recognition for different national messages when Guinness wanted to be a global brand with one message.

For Ireland, however, this was yet another sign that people revered a Guinness from the past that they knew and cherished. They were in love with an image of Guinness, yet the brand had shunned them in favour of trying to attract people who had yet to fall in love with anything at all. From 1995 to 2002, the Guinness communications agency for Ireland had been based in London. HHCL was an extraordinary agency that had won awards for groundbreaking ads for such brands as Tango, but did it ever work out what it was to be a Guinness drinker in Ireland? It did some great advertising, but arguably not for Guinness.

According to Mark Ody, 2001 saw two defining leaps. The first was the launch of "Believe," a global communications campaign with Irish connections. The second was the vast amount of work Guinness has done and is still doing on quality in Ireland, as we'll see later. They needed to happen. HHCL had failed to halt the decline in Draught Guinness sales.

When Guinness cut down its worldwide agencies to two, HHCL lost the account to Dublin-based agency Irish International, part of the BBDO group. In its first year, this new agency was to astonish Guinness with its achievements for the brand worldwide.

IRISH BELIEF

As we have seen, the scramble to create the first ads for the international "Believe" campaign was fierce, but won by Irish International. "Free-in", that very Irish reflection of inner strength, was the first TV execution. It was screened in Ireland and the UK in February 2002, before moving to Australia and the US; in so doing, it becoming the first Guinness ad ever to be broadcast across markets. It heralded the advent of the global brand, and it came from Ireland.

In the UK, the early "Believe" ads seemed to be positioned as communications that encouraged young men to find self-belief within themselves. A hurling player prepares to take a crucial penalty. A young man is determined to rescue Guinness from a pub surrounded by lava, and walks barefoot across it. In Ireland, Tommy Kinsella, head of advertising at Guinness, said the "Believe" ads marked a change of strategy aimed at encouraging Guinness drinkers to remain loyal to the brand. Same ads, different focus. At first, anyway.

In 2003, "Swimblack" was shown for the first time in Ireland, having been edited to include the line "Believe" at the end. First shown in the UK in the late 1990s, "Swimblack" features a swimmer determined to complete his annual race against the clock while his Guinness is poured, surges and settles. Then Ireland began to diverge from the UK. The third execution of the "Believe" campaign, "Tom Crean," was shown only in Ireland.

Tom Crean
Irishman Tom Crean explored the Antarctic with Scott and Shackleton, and was a vital member of their teams. During one expedition, he walked 35 miles in a raging blizzard to get help to rescue his colleagues. In the worst conditions imaginable, Tom Crean showed that you need inner strength to draw on.

This ad was the last of the "Believe" series to be made, and had that feeling of Irish tradition to it. Unfortunately, the idea of

"Believe" was in trouble with the Irish advertising authorities. Irish International, responsible for two out of the three ads, was finding it increasingly difficult to portray the connection between the beer and the action. To those who made the rules, it looked as if you needed a Guinness to be able to convert a free-in and walk 35 miles across the Antarctic. It didn't matter that Guinness was only trying to show that the kind of people who drink Guinness are those who have inner strength when they need it. To understand the significance of this, you need to be aware of the power of the anti-drinking lobby in Ireland – and the growing worry in all the more developed markets that the drinks industry will suffer the same fate as the tobacco industry and become mired in litigation and blame.

PURE QUALITY

Fortunately for Guinness in Ireland, a second stream of advertising was running concurrently with "Believe," and was based on the Guinness approach to quality.

The story begins with the fact that the single biggest driver of purchase in Irish pubs is the quality of the pint. As many as 85 percent of men claim to judge it by sight. Guinness needed to project quality in pubs – so much so that the issue reached the front pages. What could Guinness do to improve the pub pint?

It had no choice but to go back to the nuts and bolts of its business, or in this case, the pipes. It came up with a five-point programme that established new trade terms with pub landlords: fresh stock in the cellar; scrupulously clean pipes; a clean glass; a two-part pour; a crafted presentation. The end result for the consumer would be that every glass of Guinness in Ireland would bear the Guinness logo and be beautifully presented with the logo facing out.

Two years later, Guinness claims the programme is delivering great results. Publicans can earn a lot of money by fulfilling the trade terms meticulously. A series of mystery drinkers visit around 13,000 outlets four times a year. If landlords get a tick for each of the five trade terms, they earn a bonus. But the incentive goes further than that. Guinness can justifiably argue that it's Guinness drinkers who keep landlords' profits up. And its new quality team now cleans Diageo's lines in every pub every 21 days.

As a result, the man in the street is again talking about the quality of a pint of Guinness. And Guinness waited until it had carried out the improvements before going on TV to shout about it.

THE MOST NATURAL THING IN THE WORLD

"The most natural thing in the world" was the theme of a major 2002 advertising campaign, a key element in the 6 million euro Guinness Quality Communications Programme. It emphasized the naturalness of the ingredients and brewing process, which has remained virtually unchanged since 1759.

"The most natural thing in the world" sounds awkward as an end-line; it's more like a brief to a copywriter to find a pithier phrase, which is why the series is more commonly known as "Pure magic." Both lines appear at the end of the ads.

The series began with two 40-second TV ads, "1759" and "45 degrees." The ads were shot on location at St James's Gate

Brewery and in Dublin city centre. Two guys in a bar, Ziggy and Bones, played by Irish actors Billy Carter and Jason Barry, tell stories about the heritage of the Guinness brand. They try to explain the mysteries of Guinness in a tongue-in-cheek way. The ads are surreal and witty, but with a grain of truth. Their purpose is to show how the unique characteristics of Guinness originated in the eighteenth century but remain to this day. With over 200 years' experience, the quality of every pint of Guinness is guaranteed to be pure magic.

In "1759," Ziggy explains the origin of the famous two-minute pour. It was the time of day when the first Arthur pulled the first pint: "17.59, a minute to six – the angelus, man! Sure, he had to stop half-way through!" In "45 degrees," the perfect angle for the perfect pour that gives Guinness its perfect head is explained by Ziggy as the result of the lumbago suffered by Arthur Guinness.

9,000

The script for an ad called "9,000," featuring Ziggy and Bones, runs like this:
"When Uncle Arthur acquired his brewery, he only took a 9,000 year lease."
"That was a bit short-sighted of him."
"Exactly."
"So what happens in the year 10,759?"
"Maybe Guinness becomes a virtual experience."
"Enjoyed without the need to touch, taste or drink at all."
"What a nightmare!"
"Horrific!"

THE THINGS THAT MATTER

The UK's advertising heritage is more epic than Ireland's. In Ireland, advertising seems to need to return to the personal

Quarrel

"Quarrel" was the first execution of the "Things that matter" campaign in Ireland, running on TV and in cinemas from December 2003 to April 2004. It features Irish actor Michael Fassbender, star of TV series including *Band of Brothers, Holby City* and *Hearts and Bones*. A man shows his character by choosing to resolve a quarrel with a good mate, because it matters. His purposeful journey across mountains and lakes is a metaphor for the struggle he goes through to achieve his goal. The ad features Irish landmarks such as Sir John Rogerson's Quay in Dublin, the Naas dual carriageway, and the Burren and the Cliffs of Moher in County Clare. The final scenes were filmed in New York.

Mark Ody explains, "The ad really gets to the heart of what is important to the Guinness drinker. It has a genuine message that has been really well received by our consumers."

Q: Is the ad in danger of taking itself too seriously?
A: This is Ireland, and there are things that matter.

side of life. The three "Believe" ads were on an epic scale. The six "Pure magic" ads were more intimate. It seems an appropriate time for Guinness Ireland to make a third defining leap by merging the two and bringing the love of tradition together with irreverence, humour and the core message of inner strength.

So December 2003 saw Guinness move away from "Believe" into this new strategy. There is no longer an issue with the advertising authorities about cause and effect. Guinness has moved to the line "The things that matter." It's saying that the kind of people who behave as if things matter are Guinness drinkers. It's an Irish expression of inner strength: Irish Guinness drinkers who have strength know what's important. Your team. Friendship. Conversation. It celebrates Irishness.

And the message Guinness Ireland is sending the world of Guinness is this: if we can celebrate Irishness, you can and should celebrate whatever it is that makes Guinness special in your part of the world. In the past three years, Guinness has come a long way, to find itself closer to home than ever. It has sought and found a global truth that serves Guinness wherever it is in the world: Guinness is a brand with a tradition like no other, a brand that is so embedded in certain cultures that it would be impossible to find a global expression that would work for local markets. Nobody has understood this better than Guinness Ireland, where people are working flat out to retain the mystery of the brand – a lesson that the rest of the Guinness world needs to follow.

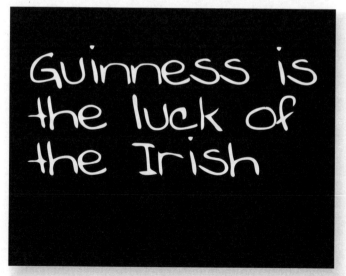

Source: Message left on the "Home" wall of postcards by a visitor to the Guinness Storehouse in Dublin, 28 November 2003

THE GENUINE MESSAGE

So what is a genuine message for the Irish Guinness drinker? It's too easy to say a reverence for the tradition of Irishness. Even tradition has to start somewhere, with newness, evolution, growth, so that someone years or centuries down the line can say "That is what is important for us to remember and bring back into our lives today."

As ever, we have to go back to where it all started, to how the company got its reputation. We've seen how the directors of Benson's came up with the phrase "Guinness is good for you" in the late 1920s. They spoke to drinkers in Dublin and found it on people's lips everywhere. And we've tried to suggest it was there because doctors dispensed it – and they dispensed it because someone told them it was true. Literary giants like Dickens, Stevenson and Thackeray said so. But these were British literary giants, not Irish. Where did they get it from? Where did the tradition start? Well, this is my theory...

UNCLE ARTHUR'S WHOLESOME BEER

Let me tell you about the real source of "Guinness is good for you." The first Arthur Guinness married into a respectable Anglo-Irish Dublin family, the Whitmores. Now, one of Ireland's foremost politicians was Henry Grattan, who was a cousin of the Whitmores. In the 1780s, as a member of the recently established Irish parliament, Henry Grattan invited his relation Arthur Guinness, now the most prominent brewer in Dublin, to speak before parliament to argue for the repeal of excise duties on beer. A straightforward move to boost profits for the family (Allfor Guineas)? It's not as black and white as that.

How did Arthur come to be involved in brewing in the first place? He and his father were each left £100 by the Archbishop of Cashel, Arthur's godfather, as recognition of his father's excellent service over the years. But hadn't Arthur been influenced by the preacher John Wesley, who visited Ireland several times and bemoaned the appalling drunkenness he found there? If Arthur's personal motto was "My hope is in God," what on earth persuaded him to open a small brewery in Leixlip with his £100? Where were his Christian values?

The truth is that they were very much intact. Beer drinking wasn't the problem; it was whiskey that was the culprit. For Grattan, beer was "the natural nurse of the people." "It is at your source," said he to the brewers, "the parliament will find in its own country the means of health with all her flourishing consequences and the cure of intoxication with all her misery."[2] When Arthur carried the day and the law was repealed, that was the goal he had in mind, not the lining of his own pocket. The Irish brewing industry never looked back. And of course Guinness became the Irish brewing industry.

So it was Guinness that set the tradition and carried it through two centuries. Down through history it came, via the powerful twin strands of popular lore and the directives of medical authorities. So when people in Dublin were asked in 1927 why they drank Guinness, they would reply with great good humour and all seriousness, "Because Guinness is good for you." But what this really means in Ireland is, "If you must drink, drink beer [Guinness] rather than whiskey."

From the very beginning there was a responsible side to Guinness drinking that has remained to this day, despite the fact that Guinness picked up whisky companies like Bell's and Johnnie Walker in the 1980s and 1990s. In fact, it speaks more loudly now than ever through Diageo, which has inherited these brands. But it was Arthur Guinness who started the ball rolling two centuries earlier. "Guinness is good for you" stems from Arthur's belief that Guinness was the wholesome alternative that would save Ireland from drunkenness through whiskey. Arthur was the original innovator, a true industrial revolutionary who transformed drinking in Ireland. And that's why the Guinness values of today – power, goodness and communion – shine through so strongly. They're built on the founder's beliefs.

So the genuine message for Guinness in Ireland is to respect the founding values that have become part of the psyche of the Irish people who have given Guinness its permanent spiritual home. That's what we mean by "tradition." Guinness has been there with the Irish people through all their traumas and transformations of the past 250 years.

HARP KEEPS GUINNESS SHARP

The Harp logo wasn't registered as a trademark in 1862 for nothing. As Protestants, the Guinness family have always had to be pragmatic in Ireland. Creating livelihoods and extending philanthropic support weren't enough by themselves to see the business through tough times. When Benjamin Lee Guinness, great-grandson of Arthur, registered the Harp trademark, he did so with his market in mind. He was a staunch Unionist who personally supervised the reconstruction of St Patrick's Protestant Cathedral in

Dublin during a major national Catholic revival. Yet he was well aware that the harp was a powerful emblem of nationalist identity that could be traced back to the popular legend of Brian Boroimhe's harp. And now Guinness had acquired that legend for its own.

There was definitely something of the original Arthur in Benjamin Lee. After the Irish Famine in the middle of the nineteenth century, national identity became very powerful. And Guinness knew how to ride the wave. The brand was rapidly becoming part of what it meant to be Irish, firmly embedded in a spiritual as well as an economic sense. The respect afforded by Guinness's position allowed Lord Ardilaun, son of Benjamin Lee Guinness, to support the notorious Captain Boycott in the Land League disturbances and get away with it. Yet he too was a great Victorian philanthropist, eventually pulling out of the business when it became a public

The politics of the brand

Guinness has operated in difficult political conditions all around the world and managed to make itself local while retaining its identity. But then it had the toughest territory of all to grow up in. Two centuries of Protestant/Catholic and Anglo/Irish strife. A beer in a country with a strong temperance movement. Owners who took their place in the Protestant establishment while claiming descent from an aristocratic Catholic line. Supporters of Catholic emancipation and opponents of Home Rule.

Even today, the Irish remain Guinness's strongest supporters, and its fiercest critics. You don't often see politics discussed as part of a brand. But it's brewed into the very essence of this one. Guinness behaves the way it does around the world because of where it comes from. Its innate Irish ability to survive stands it in good stead as a global brand anywhere.

company and putting a lot of his money into slum clearance, the building of new homes in Dublin and other projects for the public good.

When Guinness introduced Harp Lager in the 1960s, it was responding to an economic threat. Having played its own part in the lagerization of the drinking public, Guinness found itself losing ground with younger drinkers who could see no reason to drink the black stuff. In the 1990s, when Guinness tried to disguise itself by ignoring its tradition and putting on young people's clothes, it was criticized, and no wonder. But it was never shunned, because it has always had a place in the hearts of the people of Ireland. It has more Adorers here than anywhere else. And Adorers are its biggest critics.

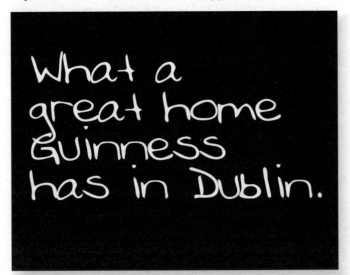

Source: Message left on the "Home" wall of postcards by a visitor to the Guinness Storehouse in Dublin, 28 November 2003

Today the harp has come through several transformations, but it still adorns the brand that represents Ireland.

WELCOME HOME, GUINNESS

So Guinness is in love with its Adorers once more. It has stopped chasing what it hasn't got, and remembered to look after what it has. And that's one hell of a lot. Those who control the brand understand that the best advertising in the world is a room full of people drinking Guinness. Just get your drinkers to do your recruiting for you.

In 2002, having lost 1 percent of its market share every year for 20 years, Guinness held its position in Ireland. And it was all down to its relationship with Adorers. Guinness is proud of itself and its drinkers again.

Equally important, Guinness understands that tradition is something that is permanently recreated through innovation. Guinness in Ireland is doing just that and showing the rest of the world the way. Nigeria may know nothing about Irishness, but thanks to Irishness, it's going to find out a lot about what it means to be a Nigerian Guinness drinker. The Irish quality initiatives are on their way to Africa.

This chapter has been a bit of a wild rover, but necessarily so. The course of Irishness doesn't follow a straight line, and can take a long time to get to the point. Before it settles, it surges, just like Guinness. And as it does so, one thing's for sure. As long as Guinness stays in its spiritual home, then its future as a global brand is assured.

Now that's Irishness for you.

Watch this space

In 2002, Guinness managed to turn around a twenty-year decline in sales in Ireland. Yet it has taken advantage of high inflation here to keep the price of its pint relatively high. It has been able to do this because the on-trade dominates the Irish market at 80 percent of sales, so price increases can be held in a way that would be impossible in off-trade and supermarket-dominated markets such as the UK. Even so, at 20 percent and growing, the off-trade has reached critical mass in Ireland. In autumn 2003, Guinness launched its new Guinness Draught In Cans in a bid to capture a share of it. Watch how Guinness in Ireland turns even more of its attention to people who drink Guinness at home.

Notes

1 "Guinness Ireland: Broadening the brand franchise without destroying the mystique," from *Brand Warriors: Corporate leaders share their winning strategies*, edited by Fiona Gilmore, HarperCollins, 1997, p. 114.
2 *The Guinness Legend*, Michele Guinness, Hodder & Stoughton, 1990, p. 10.

Guinness in Ireland

ONWARD
POWER
& AFRICA

5

A Guinness truck crawls toward a crowded crossroads in downtown Accra, capital of Ghana. A gloved policeman is stopping streams of cars and waving others on. Suddenly he turns and spots the truck. His face lights up. Frantically, he waves it through, ensuring its swift passage. As it passes, he raises his arm, abandons official decorum and yells, "The power!"

As well he might, because in certain African markets, Guinness commands the kind of respect it is normally accorded only in its country of origin. But there's nothing Irish about Guinness in Ghana, or Nigeria, or Ivory Coast, or Kenya, or Cameroon. As well as being African, these countries share two other things in common. They're five of the top ten Guinness markets in the world, and they're all under the advertising influence of Michael Power.

MICHAEL POWER: THE FIRST AFRICAN TV ACTION HERO

In the UK, back in the late 1980s, people used to ask "Who is The Man with the Guinness?" In the Africa of the new millennium, people are under no doubt who personifies Guinness for them. Michael Power is the first African TV action hero. A leader, in control, a man with massive integrity, a force for good. Launched at the turn of the century, he's now on his third TV series. With him, Guinness broke the mould in Africa, where traditional boundaries between advertising and entertainment had been strong. A product was a product to be sold, and entertainment was entertainment to be enjoyed. But Guinness put the two together, moving Michael Power from TV ads to a role in Guinness TV, its own mini-TV channel, and his own full-blown movie.

Michael Power

Where did he come from? He was invented as a character by the ad agency Saatchi's, who tapped into the African notion of the love of a hero. At the time of the advertising pitch in 1998, Saatchi's told Guinness that it could expand Michael Power from TV and poster ads into TV programmes and movies. Even the best agencies don't just come up with ideas out of the blue; even The Man with the Guinness wasn't conjured out of thin air. The right people at the right time drew together the strands of research and perception to come up with a creative answer that captured the public's imagination. OK, Saatchi's had 200 years of Guinness activity in Africa to draw on. But it quickly turned its insights into an African dream come true for Guinness.

But it's not as black and white as that.

IT ALL STARTS WITH FES

Just why is Guinness such a strong brand in Africa, and how has it managed to build up loyalty over years of contrasting economic and political fortunes? It all starts with FES.

In 2002, I wrote a script for an stage performance at a Guinness global brand forum in Jamaica celebrating the bicentenary of FES. In many respects, the story of Guinness in Africa is the story of Foreign Extra Stout. The Guinness variant with a distinctive bittersweet taste that's half as strong again as Draught Guinness is virtually the only kind of Guinness you can get in Africa. And right on that 200th celebration came the startling news that the company now sells more Guinness in Africa than in either Great Britain or Ireland. And who should arrive at the beach on a jetski, brandishing a magnum of champagne laid down in the 1950s in anticipation of just such a moment, but Michael Power!

We turned the script into a video entitled "You've got the bottle." It's a highly appropriate statement for African Guinness drinkers. Wherever they drink it, their FES comes out of bottles. It's strong and powerful and can take a bit of nerve – as I found myself when I drank my first few bottles. Before Guinness commissioned me to write about 200 years of FES, I'd never even heard of this version of the black stuff. Then it took all my efforts to get hold of some. It's not on sale in the usual UK outlets, which only added to my anticipation. But when I finally found some, was I in for a shock! It wasn't the creamy Draught Guinness I was used to. What hit me was the bitter-sweet burnt chocolate taste, like no other beer I'd ever known. And you could feel its strength in the first few swallows: 7.5 percent alcohol by volume. How much of this could you drink? One thing was for sure – I could get very used to it if only I could get hold of the stuff.

African genuineness

If we set aside the Draught Guinness sold in South Africa, the continent of Africa is 100 percent FES. This is the most widely available beer in Africa. The earliest exports were recorded in 1802, to the Caribbean. Africa first entered the books in 1827, when Sierra Leone received a small shipment. By 1914, South Africa was Guinness's third-biggest export market. A myth arose that diamond prospectors used Guinness to test whether gems were genuine, as only a true diamond could shine through that Guinness darkness.

In 1949, Guinness Nigeria was set up to import and market Guinness in what was already a big market. By the mid-1950s, a quarter of a million hectolitres of FES were being sold overseas, but newly independent countries were starting to impose import duties to protect their local industries. Despite the recent failure of its first overseas brewery in New York, Guinness knew it was only a matter of time before it began to brew in Africa.

THE AFRICA BEHIND MICHAEL POWER

Africa deserved the kudos of championing the 200th anniversary of Foreign Extra Stout. Its 40 Guinness markets (out of a total of 150 worldwide) collectively represent the company's biggest-selling market. FES is brewed in 24 of these countries, and Guinness is the number 1 or 2 player in most of the large economies. In the West African states of Ivory Coast, Ghana and Nigeria, as well as East African Kenya and French-speaking Cameroon, Guinness has sales volumes that would make other market managers blush simultaneously red with shame and green with envy. The year-on-year trading profit growth that Africa has delivered since 1985 is sensational. Yet it's still growing, and has some way to go.

If it seems odd drawing comparisons between the continent of Africa and a national market like the UK, there is a point to be made. Many more millions live in Africa, but consumption of Guinness per head is low. Average earnings are not very high, and in both Nigeria and Ghana, a bottle of FES is twice the price of premium lagers. It can take a worker half a day to earn the price of a FES. So this is a luxury purchase for a lot of people in Africa, who often drink locally made hooch or palm wine. In Nigeria, counterfeiting is a problem; people sell much weaker stouts with Guinness labels and tops.

Guinness is expensive, but they drink it. There must be a very good reason. Actually, there are several. And here we're getting into the realm of myths and legends – which, as we're talking Guinness, seems inevitable.

Source: Message left on the "Home" wall of postcards by a visitor
to the Guinness Storehouse in Dublin, 28 November 2003

MYTHS AND LEGENDS

The brand has learned to take advantage of the strange and
wonderful functional associations people make with the beer
in the vast continent of Africa.

Powerful, bittersweet, strong, heavy, caramel, burnt,
tonic... these are just some of the various attributes of
Foreign Extra Stout. They go well with Africa, which is why
Guinness avoids the problems it has had in Ireland and
Malaysia, where it can be seen as an older man's or the
previous generation's drink. Its vitality and potency are still
celebrated in folklore. "There's a baby in every bottle" is one of

144

the unofficial phrases from Africa, based on the rumour that women buy a bottle of FES and stick it in the fridge for their husband to find as a signal that they're up for a bit of how's your father.

FES is strong in flavour and in alcohol. It's stronger than lager and has a higher perceived value. Medicine shops in Cameroon sell it for its health properties. Throughout Africa, the old "Guinness is good for you" theme is very powerful. Women take it once a month. People say it cures malaria and piles. In Mauritius, where manual labour is gradually giving way to a service culture, they believe you shouldn't drink more than a bottle a week or it'll thicken your blood and you'll have a heart attack. (Unless, that is, you're a manual worker.)

Drinkers in Africa have always seen Guinness as more than just a beer. Unlike lager, it was nutritious: it had food value as well as social value. Over the years, it was inevitable that a mystique would grow up around the brand and enable it to command a premium price in the market.

If I haven't given you enough reasons why Guinness is more expensive than other beers in Africa, here are some mundane ones. Import duties on raw materials can be high. Most raw materials are expensive.

If this is the way Africans drink Guinness today, then it's down to decades of cultural reinforcement. In the past, Guinness was quite happy to hear Africans speak about the brand in functional terms. It was new to many markets in the 1960s and 1970s, yet it came with myths attached – cultural associations picked up from other African countries.

But no brand survives on myth alone. Guinness must have done something extra to mean as much as it does to Africans. It's not just taste, strength and value. There's a feeling of partnership.

THE SPIRIT OF PARTNERSHIP

If we look at Guinness in Africa today, we can see this spirit of partnership in two areas: first, in the way that Guinness is brewed and owned by the people in the markets; second, in the way that Guinness works with communities on projects crucial to their health and welfare.

Guinness is not a big foreign brewer that dumps beer into the markets and destroys local businesses. It brews in those markets. Its beer is taxed at source, as are the thousands of local people who work to produce the beer they and others consume. Critics may argue that the last thing people in Africa need is alcohol; water should come first. Nobody recognizes this more than Guinness. Its beer prices may be high, but it ploughs back some of its profits into various kinds of projects in the communities in which it operates.

These two factors alone don't qualify Guinness for exemplary global citizenship, but its activities are best judged by the people who benefit from its jobs and healthcare initiatives rather than by eco-activists running around Washington and London with sticks and placards. Much of Guinness's African business is created in Africa by African people. And a useful part of it stays there and works on behalf of African people.

MUTUALITY

Nigeria and Malaysia were chosen for the first overseas brewing operations because high Guinness exports proved the existence of a healthy market. Guinness commissioned its first overseas brewery in Ikeja, Nigeria in October 1962. From the beginning, the overseas brewing operations recognized the need to empower local people as partners. A Guinness board member, the first Lord Iveagh, got it right years before when he said: "Guinness cannot expect to make money out of people if it does not enable them to make money out of Guinness."

The Ikeja Brewery, Nigeria

The 1960s and 1970s were a crucial time for Guinness and FES. Success could be built only on partnership, on a good deal for both sides. What an innovative business concept!

AND PARTNERSHIP WAS BUILT BY LORD BOYD

It took a man with huge influence and charisma to ensure that mutual interest was the founding principle for Guinness operations overseas – a man whose glittering career had combined politics with service to Guinness for nearly 30 years.

Alan Lennox-Boyd was first elected to the Guinness board in 1942, but resigned to take office as minister of state for colonial affairs in Churchill's government of 1951. As full secretary of state in Eden's government of 1955, he was instrumental in granting independence to many British colonies. When he rejoined Guinness in 1959 as joint managing director, the company benefited immensely from his political acumen and personal friendships with post-independence leaders.

Lord Boyd, as he soon became known, immediately began an active programme of overseas investment that no British brewer has pursued before or since. He was optimistic about the future prosperity of Commonwealth countries. Some of his colleagues on the board viewed his policy as risky, especially in Dublin, where substantial exports were to be replaced by overseas production. But Lord Boyd knew that the success of newly independent nations would depend on their economic performance, and recognized that the creation of local brewing operations would benefit both Guinness and the countries concerned.

Sold overseas, brewed overseas
By the time Lord Boyd retired in 1967, over 40 percent of the Guinness sold overseas was brewed overseas. After Nigeria in 1962, Guinness Overseas Ltd oversaw the building of foreign breweries in Malaysia in 1965, Cameroon in 1969, Ghana in 1971 and Jamaica in 1973. It entered into contracts with other brewers in Australia, Kenya, New Zealand, Trinidad and South Africa, which had been one of Guinness's big export markets. Indeed, Africa was taking off. But the 1970s were when Guinness really began to make the difference that binds Africans to the brand today.

BREW BEER, MAKE MONEY, HAVE FUN

After the great leaps of the 1960s, the next decade proved a tricky one. Overseas countries were seeking a larger share in foreign-owned companies, and local staff started to flex their

Lord Boyd and Dr Azikiwe share a glass at the opening of the Nigerian Guinness brewery in 1963.

muscles. Former head of advertising Alan Wood was now managing director of Guinness Overseas Ltd. He managed to pilot the company through the difficult 1970s, and identified five reasons for the success he'd inherited in Guinness's overseas markets.

The first was Foreign Extra Stout itself. Its distinctive character and strength seemed to suit hot climates. The second was the favourable response of local governments. They encouraged inward investment because Guinness enabled them to tax the product at source, thereby creating revenue to assist national development. Third, Guinness offered proper jobs to local people. Training schemes were set up and agreements were made to localize every post within ten years. Fourth, Guinness retained control of the presentation and marketing of its product even when it was produced under contract brewing. In this way, it laid the foundations for the creation of a global brand: marketing was consistent across the world, while individual markets still received individual treatment.

The fifth and some would argue the most important reason was the invention in 1962 of Concentrated Mature Beer, now known as Guinness Flavour Extract (GFE). Created by two Guinness scientists, Laurence Hudson and Owen Williams, it was first used in 1968 to brew Guinness under licence in Mauritius.

When he retired in 1979, Alan Wood described his philosophy as: "Brew some beer, make some money, have some fun." This legacy was a great basis for the partnership that is Guinness and Africa.

AFRICA TAKES OFF

Together, political expertise and the invention of Guinness Flavour Extract enabled Guinness to open up the whole continent of Africa in the 1960s and 1970s. In time, the African brewers became major brewers in their own right and helped develop the Guinness brand of today.

The 50 percent premium that Guinness commanded allowed both Guinness and the licensed brewers to make attractive profits and encouraged more brewers into the fold. Licensed brewing took off, allowing Guinness to move into 24 markets in Africa. But how did it manage to capture such good market shares, for instance, 30 percent in Mauritius?

Source: Message left on the "Home" wall of postcards by a visitor to the Guinness Storehouse in Dublin, 28 November 2003

The main reason is that Guinness was one of the few companies to look outward at a time when other industry players were consolidating their home market.

STAYING THE COURSE: THE NIGERIA STORY

In Nigeria, Guinness took off during the civil war in the 1960s. The soldiers spread it around the country as they moved. In many ways, Guinness's experience in Nigeria is its story in Africa in a nutshell: a great learning ground for everyone associated with the brand that remains so today.

The key fact is that Guinness stayed in Nigeria (and Africa) and invested when others were pulling out. By the early 1980s, there were three Guinness breweries in Nigeria, at Ikeja, Benin and Ogba. Yet although the economy was surging and the naira was at parity with the pound, there were rumours that Guinness wasn't doing very well. When the economy did start going down, Guinness lost two-thirds of the market in a decade. What should it do: invest for the future, pull out, or what? It stayed through the bad times. It had faith in itself, its beer and in the communities where it operated.

In 1992, Guinness spent £15 million directly in Nigeria, a step that others would never have taken. Remember, this was a company fresh out of the Distillers affair in which taking risks had brought about its undoing. But because Guinness had come to understand and commit to the Nigerian market over time, it did not see the investment as a risk. It has invested continually in the market over time, and the results speak for themselves. The huge investments reap great benefits: improved productivity, quality, financial results, volumes and market share.

Today, Guinness Nigeria is a confident and successful company operating to international standards. As the economy improves and stability increases, the market potential grows. In fact, the big issue is how much to increase production capacity to meet demand. Guinness can't make Guinness fast enough.

GUINNESS IS NIGERIAN

Business development is one thing, and what consumers think of the product quite another. How does this corporate stuff translate into the behaviour of the individual Africans who drink the beer?

In many African markets, people recognize Guinness as a local brew. In Nigeria, Guinness is Nigerian; just you try telling them otherwise. For a start, it's brewed there by Nigerians, and has been for decades. Next, it's Foreign Extra Stout, not like the Draught Guinness we get in Britain. Last but not least, it's got its own special flavour. The Nigerian government has long made importing barley too expensive for brewers, so the local breweries use sorghum instead. The result is a more bitter flavour that Nigerians love. They see it as unique, better even than the Guinness from neighbouring countries.

Nigerians who travel abroad don't regard Draught Guinness as the real stuff at all. So Nigerian FES is imported into London, or wherever there are big Nigerian communities. I've picked up bottles myself in a Shepherd's Bush grocery. Nectar. You won't catch me saying, "But you know it tastes much better in Dublin." When confronted with that old chestnut, I simply reply, "But you should try it in Lagos." Even though I've been nowhere near.

GUINNESS'S EVOLUTION IN AFRICA

Today, Guinness is happy to cherish certain beliefs about the function of the beer while letting others disappear into the wide blue yonder. But as we've seen in Ireland, Guinness myths don't just disappear; they change into something else. We get a modern interpretation of an ancient idea. In Africa, Guinness is encouraging this evolution, and Michael Power's role is to make the brand less functional and more sociable. If it's associated less with a stimulant to conception and more with drinking with friends after work, so much the better.

In West Africa more than in East Africa, FES has already developed in that social way. It's great for weddings, and is often served to all the top guests. The family is immensely important, and having a huge celebration, inviting as many people as possible and being able to afford to give them all Guinness confers great prestige. FES is integrated into the culture through the way people work and live. It's part of the history and heritage.

Much of Africa is Muslim. Guinness does not give up on the world of Islam; it embraces it. Not in any exploitative sense,

But what about Muslim Africa?
The fundamental human needs on which Guinness is based are most readily apparent in Africa: when you're tired, you want to recharge. This accounts for the success of Malta Guinness. As a non-alcoholic energy and health drink, Malta's key benefit is that it revives you, restores you to your best, physically and emotionally. It was launched in the 1970s and is sold in the Caribbean and Malaysia as well as Africa, targeted mainly at Muslim populations. In Cameroon, Ghana and Nigeria, it sells over three-quarters of a million hectolitres. Around the world, it's bigger than Extra Stout in terms of volume.

but because it's been in Africa long enough to understand how different cultures work and what is expected of it.

TWENTY-FIRST-CENTURY MAN WITH THE GUINNESS

With Michael Power, Guinness is trying to represent power and goodness in ways that are more appropriate to the times. Saatchi's persuaded the Guinness Africa team to move away from the functional benefits of FES, which aren't really credible any more. After Guinness had established a firm base through its investment in the 1970s, 1980s and 1990s, he gave the brand a fresh kick by making it sociable and relevant to young Africans. The crucial point about him is that he represents existing values – physical strength, self-assurance and sincerity – but also brings new ones. He's stylish and intelligent, helping to make Guinness forward-looking and aspirational. It's a winning formula: although specific to African markets, it ties in with the Guinness global brand vision of inner strength.

INNER STRENGTH IS MADE FOR AFRICA

One of Guinness's great achievements in Africa is managing to build a brand of so much heritage by successfully adapting its brand values to the changing world. "Where you have a heritage and a belief in a brand," says David Hampshire, head of Guinness Africa, "there is inestimable worth in the brand, providing you can keep it fresh. That's the job Michael Power is doing for us in Africa."

Africans admire strong, confident men. Guinness is seen as black, strong and powerful. If Guinness is able to describe itself as the brand of inner strength in Europe, it can do so in Africa too. In a sense, it's even more relevant in the tough world of Africa, with its distinctive values and needs. Seeing these needs helped Guinness and Saatchi's develop the original insight that young men want to bring out the strong, confident person they believe lies within.

DEVELOPING THE POWER

Anyone interested in developing a brand idea can learn from Guinness's work on Michael Power in Africa. It was never just a case of creating fantastic advertising and getting it on the networks. The task was to make sure that all the functional benefits associated with the brand in Africa were channelled into something more emotionally resonant and relevant to the way people live now.

The first TV series started off with a number of linked four-minute adventures. Though it was successful, the feedback suggested people didn't get the link between Guinness and power. So Guinness supported the series with the phrase "Guinness brings out the power in you." The implication was clearly "brings out the Michael Power in you." Even in Africa, there was controversy over whether Guinness was creating a causal link between the product and inner strength. If people weren't getting the link, the second series had to be more connected.

BEYOND ADVERTISING

What a problem Guinness had! It had run four long ads on TV networks, but it needed to develop its advertising concept, and in a sense take it beyond advertising.

Why not make its own TV programme and do whatever it wanted?

Thinking big has always been a strength of Guinness Africa. How could it blur the boundary between advertising and entertainment even further? It was uncharted territory, but Africans love storytelling, and many markets suffered from a lack of quality TV. A gap in the market? You bet.

INNER STRENGTH ON THE BOX

When Guinness started looking at the concept of inner strength TV, it didn't know how to make it work. It devised a programme in three slots. The first was about people who have overcome great obstacles. The second was a documentary about people of manifest inner strength such as Nelson Mandela. The third was a movie featuring well-known American stars of Hollywood films not often seen in Africa. Julia Roberts put in a sterling performance as a committed young law student whose inner strength wins through when she finds herself running for her life in *The Pelican Brief*. Michael Power features in the programme, but doesn't run it. Guinness TV is an idea bigger than him. And it takes a bigger idea than Michael Power to develop Michael Power.

With TV Africa as the host beaming the programme out by satellite to Nigeria, Cameroon, Ghana, Ivory Coast and Kenya, Guinness TV goes out on prime-time TV between 8 and 11 p.m. on Sundays in English-speaking markets and Fridays in French-speaking markets. Guinness is able to fund this expensive venture through the advertising slots available during its own programme.

THE POWER ON GUINNESS TV

With its own format, Guinness could broaden Michael Power from the original four-minute advertisements. Now the focus shifted to drama and dialogue, taking on a more contemporary feel. Michael Power talks to you as a voiceover, or you see him talking about subjects you can relate to: music, wedding ceremonies, football. "One man embodied the dignity, the integrity and the raw uncompromised talent to leave a mark like no other – Pele!" It may look and sound rather naïve to those of us from more developed markets, but this was revolutionary stuff for Africans.

Guinness learned so much so quickly from this novel kind of marketing that when it developed a third series for Michael

The million-dollar challenge

In the early stages of the 2002 Soccer World Cup, Ireland met Cameroon. Guinness saw the match as an opportunity too good to miss. To demonstrate its belief in African soccer, Guinness Africa committed a US$1 million fund to any African team that brought home the World Cup. Half would go to the players themselves, to reward their skill and effort; the other half would go to local grass-roots sports projects.

The challenge was intended to celebrate the growth of Guinness in Africa, especially in the smaller markets. As most people outside Africa knew nothing of the company's involvement there, it had to be careful not to be seen as exploiting poor countries and not to confuse people about its Irish heritage. Few companies could have pulled this off. But Guinness could also point to its African heritage, founded on the strength of its partnership with the continent.

Guinness has a long association with African soccer, even sponsoring the captain of the Cameroon national squad. OK, so no African team got beyond the quarter-finals, and the million wasn't won. But the incentive was no sham. Guinness continued to support the sport locally. And after all, the challenge had been about winning. Winning is about self-belief, and Guinness is a beer that people associate with self-belief – a thought that stands as strong in Africa as it does in Ireland.

"Too Much Water"

Power, it found it could move him on even further. There's more realism in the next two dramas, "Race" and "Too much water." They help Guinness communicate tactical messages around real contemporary events, as it did by running a soccer ad during the 2002 Soccer World Cup.

GETTING GUINNESS CLOSER TO PEOPLE

Focusing on contemporary events was one thing, but getting closer to people was the ulterior motive. Saatchi's had the inspiration to shoot the ad dialogues in the actual markets where they were broadcast. Even though Michael Power got mobbed once or twice, local filming added a huge amount of relevance and a great inducement for more consumers to associate with the brand.

This time, Michael Power helps bring out inner strength in other people, building on the brand as a sociable drink. Heroes work for the benefit of others, not just themselves.

Michael Power now prompts specific occasion-based behaviour such as drinking after work. There seems no end to the possibilities.

The three Michael Power series have been a phenomenal success in pushing people along the drinker's journey. Whenever he enters a market, Guinness makes a huge leap of growth. And after TV, there's usually a movie...

MICHAEL POWER THE MOVIE

Once he'd been in the market for three years, Michael Power was ready for his big break. Guinness was poised to use him for the next step in engagement and awareness. *Critical Assignment* is about African strength and pride, and has a powerful theme that works well with the Guinness community initiatives Power has promoted. Michael Power is an internet journalist who wins an award for his work on clean water in Africa. There's conflict with the government and dodgy arms dealers; there's a coup; there's corruption. It's arms versus water. Michael Power helps water win through.

The movie was released in February 2003 with massive screenings in several markets. It has given Guinness the opportunity to develop the character; you see more of Michael Power and how he lives. It's only been shown in premier screenings so far: in major bars and big-screen venues. The idea is to create a Guinness environment in which people watch a big event and participate in it. Guinness reaches hundreds of thousands of people in this way. The next stage is to broadcast it and put it on DVD. Once it's on DVD in Africa, it will be everywhere.

"Critical Assignment"

SOUTH AFRICA IS DIFFERENT

But Africa is many markets, not just one. Kenya is as different from Nigeria as South Africa is from both. How has Michael Power worked across markets, and what can he teach other brands looking to do the same?

The truth is that Guinness has put in a vast amount of work to achieve a global vision for its brand, even though the Guinness sold in Africa is very different to that in the UK and

Ireland. Inner strength works particularly well in Africa. Just add local consumer insights to this theme, and Guinness can fine-tune each and every African market. The company deliberately makes the ads in Nigeria feel Nigerian, even though they feature international actors. In Kenya, they prefer more sophisticated ads, so that's what they get.

As markets become more sophisticated in their recognition and acceptance of advertising the Michael Power way, Guinness has found it can move the materials from the functional to the emotional to make them more about inner strength. But that's harder in Kenya than in Nigeria. And in South Africa, it doesn't work at all.

Truth and reconciliation

Guinness set up its licensing agreement with South African Breweries in 1964, at a time when it was growing all over Africa. From the beginning, it had sought to reach the black population. Yet sales over the next few years were almost exclusively to the ruling white European minority, largely because SAB was uncooperative about marketing Guinness in black townships. Because of this and technical brewing problems, the relationship between Guinness and SAB became strained. By 1970, sales had slipped and both sides were dissatisfied.

At the same time, the South African problem became urgent. The Organization for African Unity began talking about boycotting companies that traded in South Africa. Lord Boyd decided that Guinness shouldn't cave in to pressure of this kind, but then Guinness was not about to lose any sales. At short notice, Guinness sponsored the England versus the Rest of the World cricket series that replaced the cancelled England v. South Africa games. By 1978, pressure had increased to such an extent that the governments of West African nations from which Guinness gained its greatest African sales now supported the OAU stand. Guinness had no choice but to stop trading altogether in South Africa.

There was no further activity until 1992. After Mandela was released, Guinness was able to set up with SAB again.

South Africa is the only country on the continent where the main Guinness variant is Draught Guinness. A big market for Guinness prior to apartheid, South Africa was lost to the company by the time sanctions were lifted. In effect, it has only scratched the surface since then. But new research has told Guinness it has a big opportunity with black consumers. The problem is reaching them: it is costly to set up Draught sales in the township bars, so the opportunity has yet to be captured.

The research yielded the intriguing finding that the best Guinness variant for the black population of South Africa would not be Draught or even FES, but Extra Stout. The main reason is that the locals are used to drinking carbonated drinks out of bottles. This calls for a different kind of campaign. Michael Power didn't work here because Guinness FES had never been available to township customers and the brand has no tradition of strength and power attached to it. Guinness needed a campaign based on the product.

Michael Power may well reappear in time, when an emotional connection is needed. Emotional connections are more enduring, but Guinness's experience in South Africa is that you need to underpin it with product messages. There's always an exception to the rule, and in the world of Guinness, it's South Africa.

OUTING AFRICA

There is no denying that Guinness has built great brand equity in Africa with Michael Power. Its approach has an assurance that is based on more than the hard work it has put in over decades. Economies are improving and the company believes that the potential for more drinking is vast. This encourages it to invest even more in Michael Power and the fun, energy and entertainment of Guinness TV. At the moment, this is still a mini-TV channel within a TV channel. What's to stop it becoming a TV channel in its own right?

So far, Guinness has grown by stealth in Africa. Nobody's noticed it. With Michael Power and Guinness TV, the brand has come out into the open, and it's going to have to stay that way. If Guinness is going to make its mark on the twenty-first century, the story of Africa may well have to become the story of the brand.

The view from here is that Guinness seems to have a powerful future in Africa. It is already the biggest market for Guinness, and the third-largest for Diageo. Guinness built its business here through a spirit of partnership that overcame difficult political problems and went about the job of building community life quietly and carefully, as it had in Ireland. Few people in Africa know anything of Guinness's spiritual home, but after decades of experiencing its power to affect their lives in many ways, from livelihoods to healthcare, perhaps they now believe that Guinness has a home in their hearts too. Compliance with corporate social responsibility aside, that is the true test of the global citizen brand today. As an African Brendan Behan might have said, "The people of Africa have done a great deal for Guinness." But Guinness can truthfully say it has done a great deal for the African people. It walks its talk here.

Any modern company laying claim to the title of global citizen can't avoid the question of human rights abuses in the countries in which it operates. For Guinness, that includes many markets, particularly Nigeria, Kenya and Tanzania. But the company has a long history of trying to build local communities through economic development. Working with Diageo and Amnesty International, it has put all the human rights assurance mechanisms into place that it possibly could. It has always followed the approach that the best thing it can do is build a brewery. There's no better way to regenerate an economy, and economic regeneration is the best way to promote social stability.

The HIV pledge

The World Health Organization has reported that only 1 percent of the millions of Africans who need anti-AIDS drugs are receiving them. The cheapest drugs cost US$300 per person per year. Administering them and monitoring patients for life make the total cost of treating each person much higher.

Furthering Guinness initiatives in Africa, Diageo announced in September 2003 that it is providing its entire African workforce with access to free anti-retroviral drugs to tackle the growing AIDS pandemic. All HIV-positive staff and their dependants will receive the drugs for life, even if they leave the company. Like Guinness with its Water of Life projects, Diageo made the decision on humanitarian and commercial grounds. John Kemp, head of Diageo Africa, said: "Some of our colleagues have died from this disease and frankly that is sufficient stimulation for us to take action....There are also commercial reasons, because these people are our employees and our consumers."[1]

THE CORE QUESTION

Ultimately, Guinness is in any market to make a profit. The best way to do that is to think globally and act locally. And it knows what it needs to achieve in Africa to make that profit. So the core question for Guinness in Africa remains a consumer question: how to encourage more Accepters and Adopters to have stronger emotional ties with Guinness.

Africa has the highest percentage of Guinness Adorers in the world, but consumption per head is low. The Guinness goal is to drive consumers along the drinker's journey toward Adorer status, then increase the Adorers' "share of throat."

Yet the price of Guinness is high, and the people are poor. There's an issue here, as well as a signal for innovation. Guinness may have been in Africa for two centuries, but it can't stay the same. The next 20 years will see how much Guinness really wants to give the people of Africa the opportunity to enjoy its beer.

In the mean time, perhaps more so in Africa than anywhere else, the strong consumer insight Guinness works from is that young men want to access the strong and confident person they believe lies within: "I want to be cool... I want to be smart... I want to be successful...I want to be strong... I want to be adventurous... I want to be inspiring... I want to be admired... I want to be good."

The Power!

Watch this space
Africa now accounts for five out of the ten largest markets in the world for Guinness by volume. But the profit the company makes in the region has so far been driven by this handful of markets. Everything has been based on the phenomenal growth of FES on the continent over 200 years. But look out for South African success in the black townships and keep an eye on Ghana and West African markets as the newest Guinness brand variant, Extra Smooth, finds its place alongside its big brother.

Notes
1 "Diageo makes HIV pledge to staff," Julia Finch, *Guardian*, 23 September 2003.

OUT THINKING GUINNESS

Leaving the Guinness Storehouse in Dublin is hard to do. The reason for the sinking sensation as you exit this shrine to the wine of the country is that you've just spent a couple of hours immersing yourself in the world of Guinnessness and Irishness. Your visit to the biggest tourist attraction in Ireland is over. It feels as though everything could be downhill from now on. What else is there to do in Dublin? (Plenty, actually.) You're outside, the oppressive brewery walls behind you. You haven't got your bearings, and it's raining. Wouldn't it be great to meet a friendly face who could whisk you back to the city's delights?

I can't be the first of the millions of visitors since the Storehouse opened its doors three years ago to think that. I've been there four times, and I feel the same every time I step outside. I forget I arrived in a taxi. Not one in sight now. There are buses in nearby roads, but I don't have a clue whether I'm facing O'Connell Street or the Wicklow mountains. I might end up in Cork and be forced to drink Murphy's. There's room for improvement here, I think to myself, almost forgetting the fabulous things I've seen and learned in the building behind me.

But then I remembered what Aine Friel, the Storehouse's marketing manager, had told me about plans to redevelop this Guinness flagship. When we'd met in the Gravity Bar on the top floor, she was fresh from the previous night's party to celebrate winning the prestigious international THEA Award for outstanding achievement as a visitor centre. Aine described some of her hopes for the Storehouse and was eager for me to put in my euroworth. Now that the Themed Entertainment Association has put the Storehouse up there alongside the

London Eye, Cirque du Soleil and Universal Studios, it seems a daunting challenge to improve it still further. Just look at the statistics: 700,000 visitors a year, 42 percent of all visitors to Dublin going through the doors, Ireland's top attraction.

What's in store?
More than beer. An ultramodern facility that breathes life into an ageing brand. A way to reconnect with young customers and use the past to prepare employees for the future. That was the brief behind the Guinness Storehouse, a seven-storey brick building originally used for fermentation and 100 years old in 2004. Lit up at night, it looks like a pint of Guinness with the cream on the top.

You get exhibits explaining Guinness's history, traditions and methods, from the way the beer's made to where it goes around the world. You can tune in to all your favourite Guinness ads, and you get a fantastic view of the whole of Dublin and beyond as you swallow your pint in the Gravity Bar. If you've a mind to research, there's the Guinness Archive. There's gallery space, function space, event space, space for more. Ralph Ardill of Imagination, the London designers of the Storehouse, said: "Guinness as a brand is all about community. It's about bringing people together and sharing stories. And Guinness stout is a great social catalyst."[1] But words don't do justice to what is actually an experience, a true work of imagination.

Having been open only since November 2000, the Storehouse has never rested on its laurels. Its predecessor, the old Guinness Hopstore, was successful enough, but didn't show Guinness in a modern light. You'd leave regretting that they don't make beer barrels like that any more.

The Storehouse, like Guinness itself, regularly updates its marketing strategies. In October 2003, "Discover the vital ingredient" was the advertising campaign it was using to persuade every Dublin visitor to visit. I was interested to note that one part of the campaign focused on overcoming time constraints that might prevent people making the trip across Dublin. The ads tried to emphasize the proximity of the Storehouse, presumably to win over awkward people like me who don't quite see it like that.

Whatever I may think about the transport arrangements, I find the Storehouse unmissable whenever I go to Dublin. Last time, when I was reacquainting myself with a building I hadn't visited for 18 months, I was lucky enough to get a personal tour with a guide called Rhonda. I was just as thrilled as I was the first time by the spectacle of the rushing water in the first section, and as fascinated by the advertising floor, where simply watching other people's reactions is half the fun. I saw things I'd somehow missed on previous visits, including the wall of cards in the "Home" section, where people left the messages you can see all the way through this book. Every time I go, I see it as more and more of an experience.

Experience
Whenever Guinness invents a solution to a pressing problem, the world moves on and gives it another. Today, the Storehouse affords Guinness an opportunity to go beyond traditional marketing, away from advertising and product promotion toward personal experience. Experience marketing is not that new in the rarified world of creative design agencies, but it is to most consumers. It's the idea of communicating stories that engage, intrigue and surprise their audience, encouraging them to get closer to the brand and create their own experience. People have already made the effort to get to the Storehouse, so why not? But it takes a world-class brand with passion to pull it off.

As I dithered outside, wondering which way to walk, I began to muse about things that would make me want to come back again and again. How about entertaining the queues on the way in? By the time you get your entry ticket, you may have been queuing right around the corner in the rain. Give me some theatre! Employ actors to move up and down the queue enacting Guinness ads or historical scenarios.

Once I'm inside, show me the real world of Guinness outside Ireland. True, I've come for the Irishness. There's no need to lose it, and I doubt whether you could if you tried. But let's see some African and Asian faces. Perhaps a small bar dedicated to Foreign Extra Stout, or some product sampling sessions. Let me taste the world of difference. You've got a world of innovation. Set up a mini-lab and show me how a widget works.

When I get to the Gravity Bar it would be great to have a choice of Guinness: any variant, in any format I want. Give me choice. And when I leave, why not put me on a dedicated Storehouse bus loop to the city centre, and pick up more people to bring back? Let the Guinness experience begin in the centre of Dublin. The Storehouse is an experience that I believe could and should be extended. As Aine said, "Visitors want to be surprised." Well, surprise me!

THE CRACK IN THE CRAIC

There's a whole room on the third floor devoted to showing people the fine line between enjoying your drink and going too far. Most of the film scenarios take a long time to get to the point. On the two recent occasions I visited the Storehouse, though there were queues outside in the rain and the Gravity Bar was heaving, there were never more than two people in this room. And they didn't linger long to get the point. The section was titled "Choice." Clearly, people had made theirs and decided the craic was elsewhere.

But excessive drinking is a serious subject that no one who likes a Guinness or two should ignore. Indeed, it's one of the biggest issues the brand has faced for many a decade. It cuts through all the building-blocks that have made Guinness so successful: great quality, inspired innovation and fantastic advertising. It has the potential to raise the brand even higher, or crumble it to dust.

So, what is Guinness's approach to responsible drinking in the face of the new prohibitionism?

THE BEER WITH SPIRIT

Though responsible drinking is just one branch of Guinness's approach to corporate social responsibility, it is the one with the greatest potential to affect the brand for good or bad. In late 2003, a huge class action was brought in the US against several drinks companies, including Diageo, for their alleged role in encouraging underage drinking. Some of the Diageo brands – particularly the vodka and "ready to drink" variants – would appear to be at greater risk from legislation than Guinness. But the new prohibitionism lumps all drinks brands together and ignores the fact that different types of alcohol affect people in different ways. It may even be out to ban alcohol altogether. Whatever the agenda, no drinks company can afford to ignore it.

A survey carried out in summer 2003 found that half the UK population believes alcohol brands should run advertising campaigns preaching responsible drinking. Two-thirds said there should be warnings on packaging about the dangers of excessive drinking.[2]

If alcohol advertising gets banned, curtailed or diverted into educational purposes for which it wasn't intended because of its perceived effects on underage drinkers, Guinness will be the last drinks company in the world to blame. The dark, bitter beer whose taste is notoriously difficult to acquire is never the first pint you order in the pub at the age of 16. Guinness isn't a drink that young people binge on. Older consumers drink it regularly, but not in vast quantities. So even a socially responsible business like Guinness needs to be careful about political correctness. Guinness Adorers won't look kindly on any attempt by the brand to be seen to be saying something that doesn't really apply.

The irony here is that the company that built its reputation as a wholesome alternative to spirits is now so bound up with spirits that its ability to advertise at all is entirely at the mercy of potential legislation once again largely aimed at the evils of spirits. Guinness is Guinness... but it's not as black and white as that. When it comes to responsible drinking today, Guinness is Diageo-coloured.

BAD TEMPERANCE

Where has the new prohibitionism come from? Is there a long-term cycle mapping the ebbs and flows of the temperance movement? It was enormously powerful in Ireland in the eighteenth and nineteenth centuries. As we have seen, Arthur Guinness met it head on. His promotion of his wholesome beer in the face of the evils of whiskey was the basis for what was to become the myth that "Guinness is good for you." Temperance succeeded in banning alcohol in the US during prohibition from 1920 to 1933. "Guinness, the one drink the bootleggers couldn't copy" ran the ad.

Temperance appears in waves. It's here again. The drinks industry, whose products many of us enjoy peacefully and responsibly, is under threat from those who think they know better.

If drinking Guinness is a crime, then baby, send me to The Hague.

Source: Message left on the "Home" wall of postcards by a visitor to the Guinness Storehouse in Dublin, 28 November 2003

THE BEER WITH THE HEALTH MESSAGE

My response to people wanting to slap an "Alcohol kills" label on my beautiful can of Guinness is "Let's get our priorities right. It's not alcohol that's killing the world, it's armaments, cancer, AIDS and famine. A drink is just a drink." But Diageo is obliged to point out that it's not as straightforward as that.

Everyone I spoke to at Guinness and Diageo refuses to see it in these adversarial terms. They agree wholeheartedly with Diageo's policy on responsible drinking – not because they want to toe the political line but because it's based on sound principles of common sense and what's socially acceptable in our times.

Every company has a duty of responsibility to the people in the communities where it operates. If you sell fire, you'd better tell people how to handle fire properly. It's the way you do it that will determine whether your brand is enhanced or diminished. These are early days. Diageo is running workshops involving all staff members in exploring the boundaries of acceptability under its own marketing code. The jury is out on the effectiveness of its policy. And attempts at communicating it externally have met with as much criticism as support.

Through self-regulation, drinks advertising has entered a new phase. It is imposing a narrower scope on itself. We are witnessing a new phenomenon: the drinks brand that says "Don't buy too much of me." The role of advertising is not to educate, but to promote. So, you know which way the wind is blowing when brands are prepared to invest in public messages that undermine the benefits of their products. Yet, in the long term, it will have to be down to education to balance the role of advertising.

THERE IS NO ALTERNATIVE TO EDUCATION

Education is society's responsibility. That means government. If governments ban advertising or insist on advertisers putting counterbalancing messages in their ads or on their packaging, they are abdicating their educational responsibilities in schools. There is nothing wrong with well-executed messages about responsible drinking. But target them at those who need them. Take them into schools where drinking is already happening. Less advertising is not the answer. More education is.

That alcoholism depends on alcohol is undeniable. That alcohol is related to many forms of illness, violence and crime is unquestionable. But it isn't simply a matter of cause and effect. The two missing ingredients that are required to get from A to B are ignorance and lack of personal responsibility. Both are matters for education, not advertising. We should encourage companies like Diageo to see that education takes place with the right people, at the right time, where it matters. With children, with developing minds and consciences, in schools. "Alcohol abuse. It's as clear as your conscience. Discuss in 500 words." And leave adults to make their own decisions.

The difficulty for society is how to ensure this education is done properly. Only the drinks companies have the money and expertise to provide powerful, creative presentations that would influence children to see alcohol for what it is: a fantastic accompaniment to adult social occasions when drunk in moderation. Diageo and other drinks companies are members of the Portman Group and the Century Council, two organizations that try to ensure the right type of alcohol education is in the right place at the right time. The Diageo Foundation, the company's charitable arm, has sponsored the production of educational materials for primary school teachers in the UK and secondary school teachers in Australia. It's all a risk, but better than anti-binge-drinking ads that won't work. Surely the secret lies in getting the brands themselves to change the drinking culture of the country over time.

MY GUINNESS, FOR GOODNESS' SAKE!

As Diageo attempts to come to terms with its future, however, there is a tendency to over-egg the politically correct cake. As an avid Guinness Adorer, I don't like to see people walking on eggshells whenever the brand's majestic marketing heritage, "Guinness is good for you," is mentioned. Something so fundamental to the brand should be treated for what it is: a wonderful slogan just right for the time in which it was produced. As were "Guinnless" and "Genius" in the 1980s, two slogans that wouldn't have made it under the current UK advertising code but played a crucial part in the development of the Guinness brand none the less.

I am not disputing that Diageo should state it makes no health claims for any of its brands – but it should not overstate it. Responsible drinking is an initiative of which Diageo should be proud, but there is no need for today's approach to responsible drinking to rewrite yesterday's approach to branding. It's like a man being jealous of his wife's previous boyfriends. All the advertising Guinness has ever done is based on its first advertising. If you deny history just for the sake of political correctness, you deny an important aspect of what your brand is all about.

Let's hope that self-regulation works, because if you bend over backward too far, you end up treating adults like children. How responsible is that? And it certainly won't do the brand any good. But the challenge is a creative one. If Diageo and the drinks industry as a whole fail to adapt to responsible drinking developments, Guinness won't get to celebrate 100 years of advertising. All drinks advertising will be banned everywhere, as it is in Malaysia. And that's one step closer to banning alcohol altogether. We'd just be left with our memories of Guinness. And I want to keep drinking my Guinness.

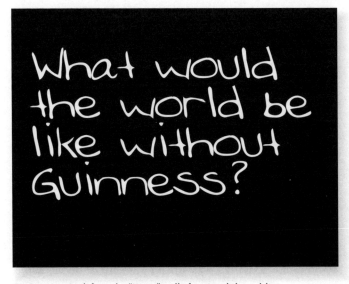

Source: Message left on the "Home" wall of postcards by a visitor to the Guinness Storehouse in Dublin, 28 November 2003

IT'S THE WAY YOU DELIVER IT

At Guinness, they talk a good line in quality and innovation, full of passion, enthusiasm and sincerity. But they know it's the way Guinness is delivered at the point of customer contact that's truly important.

During the 1990s, Guinness ran a "Perfect Pint" programme to educate bar staff and customers about the importance of the two-part pour. AMV translated the idea into effective UK advertising with "Good things come to those who wait." If you don't remember the end-line, you'll remember the surfer or the swimmer. These ads are fairly recent, yet it's still not that common to get a properly poured pint in the UK.

Even in Dublin, where Guinness is able to do far more to educate bar staff both in pubs and at the Storehouse, I've had poor pouring experiences: Guinness slopped over the side of my glass. Served in a Heineken glass alongside oysters on a plate. Even in the Storehouse Gravity Bar I've been served my pint in a glass without a Guinness logo. It's a sin. (But they were busy.)

And since Guinness is more than a beer, the way it delivers community support is equally important. You can spend a lot of money on lavishly printed corporate citizenship reports, but your actions have to live up to your words. A recent report in the *Guardian* that was mostly positive about Diageo's community activities was uncomplimentary about some Guinness work in Nigeria.[3] Local staff seemed to be making claims about non-existent water projects. True, journalists do seem to hunt out bad news even when there is a wealth of good work to look at. And not many journalists seem to understand Guinness as a brand outside Ireland and the UK. But a global citizen brand has to sing from the same hymn sheet wherever it touches the world.

In the UK, we're not as reverent about our perfectly poured pints as they are in Ireland. We're not as aware of Guinness community initiatives as they are (or ought to be) in Nigeria. Yet we've certainly taken to Guinness Extra Cold, and we cherish our widget-enabled freedom at home. And we love our advertising and still have great expectations of it. It's not our fault; you made us like this, Guinness. We were never too sure about the "Believe" ads you showed us. But we loved the recent "Perfect match" ads during the rugby World Cup. And now we're glad to see that "Out of darkness comes light." We'll tell you what we think of it one of these days.

The perfect match

In late 2003, Guinness was able to step away from "Believe" through the ideal opportunity of the rugby World Cup. Guinness has long had an association with rugby followers, having sponsored the Six Nations championship, London Irish rugby club and indeed the 1999 World Cup. In 2003, however, Guinness chose not to sponsor the tournament. Instead, it directed its resources into some creative and effective advertising in England called "The perfect match." Ads successfully combined the black-and-white body of the Guinness pint with silhouetted crowd scenes and the noisy atmosphere of the game. In a tough regulatory climate where it is increasingly difficult to associate drink with sport, Guinness showed what a strong relationship it has with rugby. Power, goodness and communion shone through. No other brand has these values; no other brand could have pulled it off. And the celebratory ad in *The Times* in London was the icing on the cake.

"The cream rises to the top" ad from the Perfect Match campaign

The Springboks need Guinness to give them strength in future

DWEEBOLUTION

As the Diageo way of brand building itself evolves to accommodate the creative needs of those who produce the ads, we may be in for a truly creative era in the history of Guinness advertising: one that works from a global perspective but still encourages creative local initiatives from people who understand their own markets. In Germany, Guinness has been advertised as the beer of character for people of character. In Australia, the focus may be on how a pint of Guinness brings people together to share great times.

There are many ways to experience Guinness. They all combine to form our view of it as a whole. And Guinness is getting it right for most of us (though only individuals can say what's true for them). The brand is respected, appreciated, loved. We have to trust Diageo to keep it that way.

Since 2001, Guinness has introduced some strong marketing, quality and innovation activities aimed at turning around declining sales – and with some success. With the sudden momentum gained from the Diageo way of brand building, the conversations at Guinness are different from those of five years ago. Instead of discussing what might be wrong with the brand, they are focusing on what's good and unique about Guinness. And markets around the world have started to grow together. Global brand director Jon Potter is enthusiastic: "Look at the balance of Guinness across the world today. In Great Britain we had several months of growth. In the US people said you can't sell a black beer in a blond market, but it's going to take off. In the last 12 months the US has grown double-digit, as have Malaysia, Singapore and Africa."

At Guinness, the brand is much more than its advertising image. As a straight advertising concept in Great Britain and Ireland, "Believe" was not as powerful as Guinness thought it was going to be. But as a global marketing concept, it was doing well in unexpected places including Asia and the Caribbean at the end of 2003. Perhaps that's because it works well as a piece of internal communication that spurs on external efforts. At Guinness, ideas never disappear. They just turn into something else.

As a company, Guinness is vastly different to what it was before Diageo. The larger organization has brought process, but also carried with it a whole group of people with the kind of experience that Guinness the brewer previously lacked. In the beginning, Diageo people who looked at Guinness expected to see a bunch of brewers stuck in the past. For Guinness, there was a natural unease at being absorbed into a larger entity. When the two started working together, Guinness had to take on a new role as a player within a portfolio, and not a major one either.

Today, with its world markets growing as fast as its confidence, Guinness is moving on again, achieving greater prominence within the wider organization. It has gone with the flow. As Jon Potter put it: "It's not the process that worries me. The issue is always creativity, because it's difficult to keep reinventing, which is what you have to do with Guinness."

INSIDE OUT, OUTSIDE IN

So here I am, someone who has seen Guinness from the inside and the outside. But I can't sit on the brand fence. After initial concerns, Guinness people are warming to the processes of the Diageo way of brand building. But I have my own concerns about the place of process, especially when it makes a louder noise than creativity.

Diageo's marketing procurement director, Alison Littley, wrote an article in *Campaign* magazine in November 2003 in which she argued that the tension between procurement departments and creative agencies hinges on a paradox: both sides want great advertising, but they can't agree on how to get it. "The problem is this: clients like arithmetic, agencies like literature."[4] But my question is: what do Guinness drinkers like?

I can only comment on what I see happening to Guinness advertising. Dweeb began in 1999. For me, the last good Guinness ad was "Swimblack," from 1998. It now takes an age for a Guinness ad to emerge, if it ever does. It isn't for want of creativity; it's more to do with ads failing to reach certain targets, goals or other criteria that seek to assure its success before it even hits the screens. And time waits for no brand.

In my time in business, I've seen lawyers and accountants getting the upper hand more often, and ruining good brand communication ideas because of their futile determination to eliminate risk. Until I see proof otherwise, I'll continue to believe that Diageo is in danger of making a pig's ear out of a silk paradox. In the mean time, I rest assured that the brand is more confident than those who ultimately decide how it should be communicated.

Guinness is a mould breaker. The brand has survived for 250 years largely because it has broken through accepted boundaries when it had to. Today, as a small part of a large organization, Guinness has to ask itself whether it has the will, never mind the ability, to break the rules when the going gets really tough. But first, hedged in by rules, it needs to determine which of them to break.

THE NOT-SO-SECRET INGREDIENT

Guinness is a beer. It's all there in black and white. But this beer brand is more than the sum of its quality, innovation and advertising. There is an extra ingredient that isn't all that hidden: passion. Many brands use that word nowadays, but it's how they behave that counts. It's the way people out there in Guinness markets throughout the world make things happen that truly personifies the brand.

Many people believe genius lies in inventing something that has never been seen before. When it comes to branding, I believe genius lies in reinvention. Why rack your brains to invent something new when you can put your passion into reinventing what you already are for a new audience in a new time? There's the genius. Remember Rutger.

According to global brand director Jon Potter: "We grow in markets where we have no right to grow. How come? It's the people. Look at the people who go out there and sell our brand. People were concerned that passion was one of the things that might be lost with Diageo – but all the benefits are still there because the passion has been retained."

Passion is difficult to pass on. You've either got it or you haven't. But there are several things from the Guinness story that other brands can learn from:

Put innovation first. Learn to strike the right balance between innovating on the quality of existing products that sell well and on the novelty of new products that haven't yet been tested. *Experimentation is essential.*

Make advertising relevant, motivating and believable for people at the time. Its truth will take the brand forward in the long term as long as creativity is allowed to flourish. *Risk taking is important.*

Carry the DNA of the brand from the first market to the 150th. Rather than transferring Irishness into Nigeria, this means staying passionately true to your traditional brand strengths and adapting them to the culture of the market you're in. *Difference is crucial.*

Recognize and celebrate the brand's hidden heroes. It's easy to focus on sophisticated products in developed markets when the profit-making parts of your portfolio lie undeveloped, in undeveloped parts of the world. *Unfashionable is fashionable.*

Behave like a global citizen. Actions speak louder than words, but in pursuing a socially responsible image, be careful not to traduce your brand's historical values. *Heritage is golden.*

Re-present the brand. In the perpetual temptation to reinvent the wheel, maybe trying to cram several square pegs into one round global (w)hole isn't the way of the future. *Complex is simple.*

Because Guinness is Guinness.

BLACK TO THE FUTURE

I started the book with a pint of Guinness on a bar, and I'm going to end with one.

Today, after two decades of Guinness drinking, you'd think I might be jaded. Not at all. I'm more in love than ever. When I enter a bar where the atmosphere is just right – not too crowded, not too loud – I still get a thrill from ordering my pint, watching it being poured slowly and carefully, contemplating the surge, thinking about my life during the settle. In the right glass, with the logo facing me and the impact on the creamy head where the last drop has fallen, there is no better sight. I'd leave it there for ever, except I can't wait any longer to take that first gulp, to taste that roasted bitter flavour once again, the taste that can only be Guinness. Oh, there are other black beers, other creamy stouts, but there is only one Guinness.

I could tell you a lot more about it. But Guinness is Guinness. Let's enjoy it.

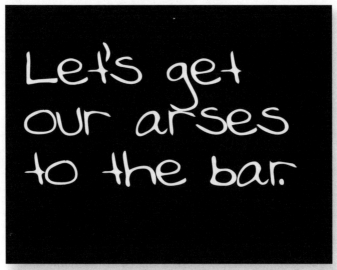

Source: Message left on the "Home" wall of postcards by a visitor to the Guinness Storehouse in Dublin, 28 November 2003

Notes
1 "Guinness Storehouse is a way to get in touch with a new generation," Scott Kirsner, *Fast Company*, May 2002.
2 "Majority support health advice on alcoholic drinks," Tania Mason, *Marketing*, 17 July 2003.
3 "Brewing a set of standards," Julia Finch, in "The giving list," *The Guardian*, 17 November 2003.
4 "The procurement paradox," Alison Littley, *Campaign*, 28 November 2003.

ALMOST 250 YEARS OF GUINNESS

1759   Arthur Guinness founds a dynasty that will control the Guinness brewery for 227 years, until 1986

1775   Arthur defends his water rights against the Corporation of Dublin and saves the brewery

1792   Before the Irish parliament, Arthur champions Guinness as a wholesome beer that will save the country from the evils of whiskey

1794   First record of Guinness being drunk in London: an illustration of a porter drinker is published in *Gentleman's Magazine*

1802   First record of West Indies Porter (now known as Guinness Foreign Extra Stout, the oldest surviving Guinness stout) being exported to the West Indies

1815   One of Wellington's cavalry officers, severely wounded in the Battle of Waterloo, attributes his recovery to the powers of Guinness

1821   Guinness Extra Stout Porter first brewed

1827   The first record of porter reaching Africa, where a certain Ed Shaw takes charge of 20 hogsheads in Sierra Leone

1836   Charles Dickens refers to Guinness verbally and visually in *Sketches by Boz* and *The Pickwick Papers*

1862   A trademark registry is set up in London and Guinness registers the Harp motif and Arthur Guinness's signature

1886   St James's Gate is the largest brewery in the world, exporting 50,000 hogsheads a year; Guinness becomes a public company in the year that Coca-Cola goes on sale in the US.

1912   A shipment of Guinness sinks with the *Titanic*

1929   First Guinness advertisement appears in the UK: "Guinness is good for you," produced by S. H. Benson of London

1934   John Gilroy designs the "Guinness For Strength" poster campaign featuring a man with an iron girder

1935   Gilroy produces "My goodness, My Guinness," featuring a zookeeper and his menagerie; the first big brewery outside Dublin opens at Park Royal, London

1942   Guinness works with the Ministry of Information to produce "Dig For Victory" and other morale-boosting wartime posters

1954   Sir Hugh Beaver launches the *Guinness Book of Records*, which quickly becomes a bestseller

1955   A Guinness ad featuring a zookeeper and sea lion is the second ad to appear on the opening night of British commercial television

1959   Michael Ash invents the Easy Serve cask system to make Guinness Draught available in pubs; Alan Lennox-Boyd ends his governmental career and rejoins Guinness as joint managing director, and the era of overseas expansion truly begins; Guinness celebrates its bicentenary as the author of *Guinness Is Guinness*... is born.

1961   Laurence Hudson and Owen Williams invent Concentrated Mature Beer (now known as Guinness Flavour Extract), enabling Guinness to eventually be brewed in lager breweries overseas

1962   Guinness commissions its first overseas brewery in Ikeja, Nigeria

1969   J. Walter Thompson wins the Guinness advertising account from S. H. Benson after 40 years, and Guinness Draught's advertising becomes distinctly different from bottled Guinness Extra Stout's

1976   The author drinks first pint of Guinness, but isn't sure

1986   Guinness merges with Distillers, changing the company ownership for ever; the Guinness Distillers affair rocks the company and eventually sends managing director Ernest Saunders to prison on charges of theft and false accounting

1987   Launch of Ogilvy & Mather's successful advertising campaign "The Man with the Guinness" featuring Rutger Hauer, confirming Guinness as the author's favourite drink

1989   Thanks to the invention of the widget, Guinness Draught In Cans is launched in Britain

1992   The Guinness family cease to be directly involved in the management of the company, although they still retain a financial interest in the business

1997   The Guinness Company joins with Grand Metropolitan to create Diageo, the largest drinks company in the world.

1998   Abbott Mead Vickers BBDO becomes only the fifth advertising agency to take over Guinness's UK advertising account in 70 years, and its new advertising campaign to promote the launch of Guinness Extra Cold, "Good things come to those who wait," features the most popular Guinness ad of all time, "Surfer"; Saatchi's, Guinness's advertising agency for Africa, invents the character of Michael Power

1999   Guinness introduces the rocket widget, enabling drinkers to enjoy Guinness Draught straight from a bottle

2000   10 million glasses of Guinness are drunk every day around the world, or almost 2 billion pints a year

2001   After 47 years of topping the listings, the *Guinness Book of World Records* is sold to the owners of Sooty and Thomas the Tank Engine

2002   The "Believe" advertising campaign is launched in the UK, Ireland, USA and Australia, and the Adam King character is launched in Asia; Guinness Foreign Extra Stout celebrates its 200th birthday as the oldest surviving Guinness brand variant; Africa is now the biggest-selling Guinness market in the world.

2003   Scientists from the University of Wisconsin prove that a pint of Guinness a day taken at meal times is good for the heart

2004   After 70 years of brewing, Diageo announces the closure of London's famous Park Royal brewery due to flat demand and over-capacity. After 27 years of drinking, the author notches up his 3,000[th] pint of Guinness and looks for more.